BEYOND
FRIENDSHIP
AND
EROS

SUNY series in the Philosophy of the Social Sciences
Edited by Lenore Langsdorf

BEYOND
FRIENDSHIP
AND
EROS

*Unrecognized Relationships
between Men and Women*

John R. Scudder Jr.
and
Anne H. Bishop

STATE UNIVERSITY OF NEW YORK PRESS

Published by
State University of New York Press, Albany

© 2001 State University of New York

For information, address State University of New York Press,
90 State Street, Suite 700, Albany, NY 12207

Production by Cathleen Collins
Marketing by Anne Valentine

Library of Congress Cataloging in Publication Data

Scudder, John R., 1926-
  Beyond friendship and Eros : unrecognized relationships between men and
women / John R. Scudder Jr. and Anne H. Bishop.
      p.   cm. — (SUNY series in the philosophy of the social sciences)
  Includes bibliographical references and index.
  ISBN 0-7914-5115-1 (alk. paper) — ISBN 0-7914-5116-X (pbk. : alk. paper)
  1. Man-woman relationships. 2. Married people—Psychology. 3. Love.
4. Platonic love. 5. Friendship. I. Bishop, Anne H., 1935- II. Title. III. Series.

HQ801 .S4417 2001
306.7—dc21
                                                                    00-067133

10 9 8 7 6 5 4 3 2 1

To
Mary and Bobby
whose support, understanding, and love made our relationship
and this book possible

CONTENTS

PREFACE

We have written this book to help others make sense of personal relationships between the sexes that do not fit into contemporary sociocultural categories. We have attempted to articulate our own relationship for over twenty years in a way that satisfies us. In developing this book, we expanded this quest to include the experience of others engaged in deep personal relationships with persons of the opposite sex who are married to other persons. Our articulation draws on interpretations of our own personal relationship, similar relationships of interviewees, relationships in literature, and popular movies. Our articulation is greatly enriched with philosophical treatments of personal relations. As we explore these relationships and philosophical interpretations, it will become evident that the relationship we are articulating is not merely an idiosyncratic one but a relationship of much wider significance and one that warrants consideration as a possibility for others and for further investigations by scholars.

We first describe and consider love relationships that foster abundant being that we and others have experienced. Then we show how this love is unrecognized in our culture in two senses. First, it is not a recognized designation that is available to couples as expectations and directions for cultivating relationships. Second, it is not recognized as a socially acceptable relationship. Next, we compare and contrast that love with the friendship and erotic love that our culture uses to articulate such relationships. We discovered that both relationships fail to capture the meaning of relationships such as ours. The love we experienced came from direct personal encounter and response to each other's presence. This dialogical love can be present in both friendship and erotic love, but since dialogical love is treated as an aspect of both relationships, neither can adeqately articulate relationships such as ours. Dialogical love is the essential meaning of relationships such as ours and in this sense goes beyond friendship and erotic love. Consequently, when asked "Is this a friendship or a lover relationship?" those in such relationships do not know how to respond. We contend that the response should be, "Neither designation is adequate! Our relationship is dialogical love."

We believe that our conclusion that dialogical love is a different way of looking at relationships between the sexes is an important discovery. Had we interpreted our relationship as dialogical love much earlier, we would have avoided many years of frustration, but we also would have missed an engrossing quest. Our quest has greatly enlivened, as well as enlightened, our years together. We have continued this quest during the writing of this book over the past several years. When we began, we did not know what conclusion, if any, we would reach through an intense focused quest to make sense out of relationships such as ours. We were surprised to discover that dialogical love well articulates these relationships. Most books begin with a conclusion and give reasons for that conclusion in linear fashion. Instead of this approach, we began with a quest to understand and articulate an unrecognized relationship that reached a surprising conclusion. After concluding that our relationship was dialogical love, we faced a difficult decision. Should we reorder our investigation to make it a linear argument supporting our conclusion or leave it as an open-ended dialogical investigation that reached a surprise conclusion? Reviewers found the open-ended approach unnecessarily confusing. But giving a linear argument would not work because we did not arrive at our conclusion by reasoned argument but through dialogical reflection and investigation of a certain kind of relationship between men and women that had not been articulated. We decided to begin with the conclusion that these relationships are best articulated as dialogical love, then to articulate that relationship and support our conclusion in the way that we arrived at it through extended dialogical investigation.

We approach articulation of dialogical love from the perspective of a relationship between a man and woman who are married but not to each other. We did not *choose* to write from this perspective. It *is our* perspective. The older we have become (we are both retired) the more we have questioned the validity of writing from the perspective of "one." Such writing implies that we can speak from a perspective that is different from ours and that we can make pronouncements that are more valid than our experience and judgment can support. We prefer writing as Jack and Anne who are situated in the world in certain ways with certain backgrounds, concerns, talents, and limitations—in short, our way of being in the world. We interpret the world from our own perspective, but we hope that what we consider and how we consider it will be of interest to others. We try not to speak for others by putting them in general categories such as heterosexual or homosexual and even man or woman. When we think together dialogically, we encounter each other as Jack and Anne, not as man and woman. But we do share with each other our experience of growing up in a male or female world with certain expectations that were often limitations. We think and write from the world as we have known it separately and together. We enlarge that world with conversation, reading, thought, reflection, and insights that expand the world as we have known it. We hope that our book will help others enlarge their world.

We are grateful to our editor, Lenore Langsdorf, for insightful criticism that helped us avoid pitfalls that would have led to unnecessary confusion and antagonism by our readers. Her criticism also took the form of suggesting possibilities that helped us focus more clearly on what has become the central theme of this book. We are especially grateful to Mary and Bobby, our spouses, for their many contributions to our relationship and to our understanding of it. In practical, concrete ways, they helped all four of us cultivate complex, unique, positive relationships in potentially difficult situations. Our appreciation of their contributions will be evident throughout the book.

Chapter 1

WHY ANOTHER
INTERPRETATION
OF LOVE?

This book is the culmination of our over-twenty-year attempt to articulate the meaning of a dialogical love relationship between a man and a woman who are married, but not to each other. We will articulate the meaning of dialogical love throughout this book by reflecting on concrete examples, seeking the meaning of this relationship in light of the thought of scholars, and by dialogue between the authors. For now, we will merely identify dialogical love as love that grows out of personal interaction that is initiated by the presence of the other and responds directly to that presence. It contrasts with "love" in which persons use each other to meet personal and sexual needs and employ cultural prescriptions to dictate the relationship between the sexes. Dialogical love is not a thing that can be used or had but is a "love that is lived in . . . and within the light of which" we live (Eliot 1959, 88).

We are attempting to initiate a way of thinking about relationships between men and women that is already coming into being in our so-called postmodern era. By postmodern we do not necessarily mean the many assertions that are now being associated with the word *postmodern*. Our meaning of *postmodern* comes from the time before most of contemporary postmodern talk. It came from philosophies of history such as those of Arnold Toynbee, Oswald Spengler, and Pitirim Sorokin. By postmodern we mean that the modern age is collapsing, and we are

1

in a period of confusion and promise much like the Renaissance. In our time, many of the traditional ways of being are being challenged and new ways are being envisioned.

The new understanding of women and their place in the world is certainly an example of such change. Looking at women in a new way requires a new understanding of the relationship of men and women. Amazingly, John Stuart Mill and his friend (and later, wife) Harriet Taylor, understood this in the nineteenth century, as did John Macmurray in the first part of the twentieth century. Macmurray developed an interpretation of personal love that called for change in the way we think of the relationship between men and women. Martin Buber and Alfred Schutz interpret ways of being between persons that imply new understandings of the relationship between men and women. C. S. Lewis and Rollo May treat love as a personal relationship and distinguish love from friendship. Caroline Simon and Robert Solomon treat intergender friendship directly and explore its relationship to love. In this book we will share the thought of philosophers who have enlightened our understanding of the relationship between men and women and will explore possibilities they suggest.

We will explore possible nontraditional personal relationships between men and women and give concrete examples of how some of these possibilities have found fulfillment. We will ask our readers to entertain the possibility of developing new relationships with persons of the opposite sex rather than the traditional ones based on sex and romance. The primary question this new direction raises is not, "Are they friends or lovers?" but "Is their relationship personal or impersonal?" Relationships that focus on fitting the designated ways of society are often impersonal—even when they are called personal relationships such as friends or lovers. In personal relationships, as we will show, persons respond to each other as they are present to each other and in ways that presence calls forth, rather than by following the dictates of societal roles. When people attempt to relate to each other personally within the confines of societal structures, they often find their personal relationships restricted and truncated by these structures. Even those who initially do not feel their relationship restricted by traditional structures often look to their personal relationship as it matures, rather than to society, to define the meaning of that relationship.

Our goals in trying to articulate the way of being that we have called dialogical love are twofold. Academically, we want to issue a call for further exploration of what we designate as dialogical love so that it can be better understood and more clearly articulated. Personally, we want to help others venture out and explore new personal relationships that go beyond traditional structures in their quest for abundant being and deep personal fulfillment.

We can speak of relationships that foster abundant being and deep personal fulfillment because we have been in such a relationship for over twenty years. We have encountered other couples who have experienced similar relationships, some of whom participated in the interviews used in this book. Those we interviewed shared the common experience of developing deep fulfilling relationships that do not fit into the accepted categories of our society—courtship, marriage, affairs, or "just" friend relationships. We did not interview persons whose friendship with members of the opposite sex were not deep personal relationships. For example, when a colleague discovered that we were writing this book, she eagerly volunteered to be interviewed, believing that study of friendship between the sexes was much needed. When we told her that we were interested in relationships that were deeply personal, she said that her relationship with her male friend was not the kind of relationship we were seeking. In our research, we discovered that friendships, such as that of our colleague, have been studied more often than we expected. These studies generally use standard social science techniques and supply quantitative and qualitative data concerning those relationships. While these studies are needed, few were significant for our investigation of the *meaning* of deep personal relationships between men and women outside of marriage.

Studies of relationships between men and women outside of marriage take place in a sociocultural context that assumes that the normal relationships of men and women are usually structured on a gender basis. Courtship-to-marriage relationships and affairs have in common that they are based on romance and sex. Relationships between men and women that do not involve romance and sex are usually referred to as "just" friend relationships. Unlike "just" friend relationships, rich personal relationships between the sexes have been overlooked. Most people are aware that "just" friend relationships can become affairs, but few people seem aware that "just" friend relationships can blossom into relationships of dialogical love. Those of us who have experienced the abundant being that can come from a deep personal relationship with a person of the opposite sex would never speak of our relationship as "just." Calling these relationships "just" friend is not only misleading; it trivializes the relationship in a way that seems like sacrilege.

Our initial focus will be on the positive fulfillment that we call abundant being that is experienced in relationships of dialogical love. These relationships are often initiated by the many opportunities that men and women have for being together in our time. We met as colleagues and the unusual amount of time we have spent together has been recognized as professionally legitimate. We have coauthored five books and numerous papers and articles in an attempt to interpret nursing philosophically. The foregoing statement can, however, be misleading in that it sounds like a professor of philosophy and a professor of nursing became related to each other in order to interpret nursing philosophically. In fact, we were close friends before we began to investigate together the meanings of nursing, practice, and caring. Our scholarly writing grew out of our friendship rather than our friendship developing from our professional work together.

Over the years, in addition to thinking about the meaning of nursing, we have attempted to make sense of our relationship. Unlike our attempt to discover the meaning of nursing, we have not, until now, published anything concerning our quest to make sense of our dialogical love. Such an exploration is so personal that it is difficult to know how to share it with others. At first, we wondered if we were alone, but we discovered that others have had relationships similar to ours and also have struggled to articulate them. Some were well-educated, some had little education; some were old, some were young; some were from urban areas, some from rural. All shared the common experience of being in a relationship that enriched their lives but had no acceptable place in our culture. We interviewed them in unstructured discussions concerning the content and meaning of their relationships. The unfolding of the interviews followed the direction given by the interviewees. For example, sexual relationships were discussed only if the interviewees chose to include them. We will include material from these interviews dispersed throughout the book to give insight into the meaning of what we call dialogical love and to make it concrete.

In addition to our interviews, we were surprised to find that some famous literary and philosophical leaders were in relationships that involved experiences and quests similar to ours. We discovered that John Stuart Mill and Harriet Taylor as well as C. S. Lewis and Joy Davidman groped for the meaning of their relationship in a way that strikes a chord with our own quest for meaning. In addition, Margaret Fuller unsuccessfully sought to develop such a relationship with Ralph Waldo Emerson. Given that Mill, Taylor, and Fuller lived in Victorian times, it seems strange that their quest would strike a chord with those of us who believe we live in a time of great liberation from Victorian restraints. Actually, we are old enough to have grown up under the remnants of Victorian constraints. Most of the younger couples we interviewed have felt few such constraints. Consequently, they initially felt freer than we to develop personal relationships between the sexes outside of marriage. Greater freedom, however, does not of itself draw out and articulate the meaning of these relationships. In fact, it is likely that those of us who have experienced restraint as well as freedom may be better situated to articulate the meaning of what we are calling dialogical love.

Articulating the meaning of relationships of dialogical love involves a personal quest for meaning. It is a difficult quest because the relationship has not been culturally defined. Since this relationship does not fit the so-called tried and true relationships of our culture, our search for the meaning of the relationship requires groping, accompanied by much uncertainty. Those involved in relationships that are not culturally defined wonder, at first, if their relationship is unique.

New lovers, traditionally, have assumed that their relationship is unique. It is well established in the literature of love that this feeling of uniqueness is characteristic of new love. New lovers proudly proclaim that their love is like no other love. Those who experience love that is not culturally recognized are not given to such proclamations. They fear that they are alone and fervently hope that others experience what they are experiencing. They are uncertain about the meaning of their relationship and are reaching out for help in making sense of its meaning. Their quest for meaning is stymied by the language of our culture that tends to falsify more than express what they are experiencing.

Articulating dialogical love requires an unusual way of writing. Most authors who attempt to articulate a new aspect of human experience in a field that has been well treated follow the traditional linear development of a line of thought. These books often begin with the authors stating their conclusion, continue by developing the argument that supports the conclusion, and conclude by testing the soundness and usefulness of the conclusion. This type of presentation is most successful when what is pursued is not highly personal and is in a field that has been treated by many others. The clarity of such articulation is often bought at the price of a loss of freshness and excitement for both the writers and the readers.

We will attempt to keep the vitality and passion we have felt in questing for understanding dialogical love by including much of our own dialogue throughout this book. Dialogue is well suited for reflecting on meaning that is initially unclear. When we began this book, we could not adequately articulate the meaning of our relationship. Only after an intense dialogical quest, involving reflection on the meaning of our relationship and those of others, were we able to articulate these relationships as dialogical love. We hope that our readers, by sharing in our quest, will come to understand why we articulate our relationship as dialogical love and see in its meaning a possibility for themselves and others. Those who want the meaning of dialogical love adequately defined in the beginning of the book and then supported by argument will be disappointed. The meaning of dialogical love will become evident as we engage in a dialogical quest for meaning throughout the book.

Our reflection will be personal in the sense that we will share from our personal quest. It will not, however, be limited to our experience and insights. We will share insights and understandings gained from those who have contributed to our grasp of the meaning of dialogical love: philosophers and other thinkers, literary descriptions and interpretations, dialogical interviews, and popular media. Our purpose for including this material in our book is to clarify the meaning of dialogical love.

Our way of thinking has been much influenced by hermeneutic phenomenology in which examples are used to clarify meaning. The examples used can be biographical or fictional or some place in between. They are used simply to better disclose meaning. We have chosen to include works that have helped us discover and disclose the meaning of dialogical love. We do not claim to have researched all the literature that could be related to such a quest. Instead we will share understandings gained from involvement in a personal quest for meaning that has evolved through our dialogue with each other and searching out authors, situations, and relationships that have given us insight into the meaning of our own relationship. We have been delighted to discover that we are not alone in living in our kind of relationship. We hope that by sharing some of our insights into the meaning of dialogical love, others may find that abundant being that we have found together.

The obvious answer to the question, "Why another interpretation of love?" is that we want to help others find the abundant being and fulfillment that we have found in a relationship of dialogical love. We offer dialogical love as a challenge to the traditional ways of relating men and women that stress differences between them, romance and sex, and distinctions between love and friendship. Persons pursuing the abundant being of dialogical love will encounter lack of recognition of their relationship in popular culture. Embedded in popular culture is an assumption that love and friendship are entirely different, mutually exclusive ways of being, and consequently, that relationships between men and women who are married but not to each other must be either affairs or "just" friend relationships. Our quest led us from popular culture to C. S. Lewis and Rollo May who interpret friendship and love as personal love relationships. Although their interpretations enlightened our quest, they also stress the contrast between friendship and love and fail to treat friendship between men and women specifically. Then, we explore the specific treatments of friendship between men and women of Caroline Simon and Robert Solomon. Although both contrast friendship with love, Solomon does indicate that a new direction is needed by

ANNE: When our thoughts, feelings, and lived body are in harmony, we can be at peace with ourselves and are more apt to be at peace with each other. Then we can be free and open to the possibility of abundant being.

JACK: Dialogical love gives depth to our personal relationship that both broadens and expands our being. That love comes from dialogically responding to the presence of each other.

ANNE: Dialogical love fosters abundant being concretely. Often when we enjoy the Blue Ridge Mountains together, our feeling of at-oneness with each other suddenly becomes an at-oneness with the whole world. The ecstasy of our being together expands and takes root in an ecstasy of relatedness to all being. With that relatedness comes a feeling of peace as I have never known it. That peace seems to me to be the peace that passes all understanding.

JACK: That peace is an excellent example of what we mean by abundant being. You experienced peace as you have never known it before, both in depth and in what it includes and you recognize that peace as good. That peace comes into being through our relationship of dialogical love.

Societal Restraint and Misdirection

"I love Japanese food and there is a place where for several years I was a regular, like I would be there two or three times a week. I really liked that place. So I came in after several years and the owner recognized me which was nice, and then he looked up and James paid for the meal because that was during a time I was helping him. And he looked up surprised and said, 'Oh, are you married?' And we both chuckled and I said, 'Yes, but not to each other.'" (Marian)

JACK: We've had similar experiences to that of Marian in which the way we relate to each other leads to misinterpretation of our relationship. Our ease of being with each other in a "we-relationship" fosters the assumption that we are married to each other.

ANNE: When people encounter an unarticulated relationship in our society, they tend to force it into the wrong category of meaning. Fear of false labeling has prevented you from honestly showing your affection for me in public in the way that you do for others. I remember how chagrined I was at my son's wedding when you hugged every woman that you knew except me. You shook my hand!

JACK: But that was early in our relationship when I was uneasy about how to relate to you in public. Later, the tension between our way of being together and normal societal expectations became one source of the humor that continually wells up when we are together. I almost cracked up in church one Sunday when one member spoke of us in a way that unconsciously implied a more intimate relationship than most church folks are comfortable with. Another quickly chimed in and said, "But, of course, they write all of those books together!"

ANNE: Our "we-talk" is perfectly acceptable when it concerns our professional relationship in developing a philosophical interpretation of nursing. But when the we-talk concerns our personal relationship with each other, eyebrows raise, and our we-talk implies that we are more than "just" friends. To most that means we are lovers.

JACK: It's not surprising that people find it difficult to accept our relationship in the small southern city in which we live and especially in the small liberal arts church-related college in which we have taught, or in the church in which we are active members. I think it would be easier to have a relationship such as ours if we lived in a big city, but I don't really think that community differences are the primary difficulty. Persons we interviewed, who were in relationships similar to ours, came from communities that varied from the East Coast to the West Coast, from the southern United States to Canada and from rural communities to big cities. Those persons experienced the same problem in finding an accepted place in society that we have.

ANNE: Marian shared your view. I asked her if she thought that living in a large city made it easier to openly develop and express

---

"When Dick died, I thought thank goodness, I'll be able to go to the bereavement group, and it'll be someplace I can talk. As soon as I started talking, everybody turned to me and said, 'What about his wife? How is his wife doing?' And it was like I didn't have a right to have grief—that it really belonged to his wife. And I thought you don't even know his wife; you know me. I've been here all this time, and now I need something. And it was like they couldn't do it. It was such a barrier that I would be grieving for somebody else's husband. And that's how they saw that. I couldn't wait to get to the bereavement group and there was no bereavement group, and there's still no bereavement group where you would probably feel welcomed if you were talking about the grief of a friend. Or the grief of a male friend especially." (Liz)

The members of the grief group apparently had assigned Liz to the category of "just" friend. Since they did not have a sexual relationship, they would qualify for the category of "just" friends in our society. But Liz and Dick certainly did not fit that category because of the quality of their relationship. Liz and Dick proclaimed their love for each other after they discovered he was dying. Unfortunately, in our society there is no way to recognize close intimate relationships between women and men outside of a sexual relationship. When someone says of a couple that they are "just" friends, the "just" implies that a lover relationship is the preferred and only accepted close relationship for men and women. When their affection for each other cannot be contained in the "just" friend category, it is assumed that they must be lovers. One purpose of this book is to reject this absurd interpretation of intimate relationships between men and women.

There is an assumption in our society that men and women have to choose between friendship and lover relationships and that a lover relationship is a preferable one. In one popular song a lover proclaims that she loves the beloved too much to be a friend. In another song a lover concludes that their love relationship ended when his lover said that they were friends. Another song celebrates the end of a beautiful friendship because a relationship of love has begun. These popular songs reflect the exaggerated view of romantic love prevalent in our society. Romantic love fosters the contention that love and friendship are mutually exclusive ways of being and that love is preferred over "just" friendship.

Romantic love is believed to be so different from other personal relationships that it has been humorously labeled as "madness." A popular song says that when you hear singing and smell blossoms that are not there, you are not mentally ill but just in love. To those outside of the love relationship, the "bizarre" behavior of lovers is often dismissed with the remark, "Oh, they're in love." That is how Romeo's friends dismissed his strange uncharacteristic behavior. Being romantic, inexperienced, and sexually over-charged, young lovers are readily transported into an ecstatic world. Although sexual attraction and the desire for pleasure foster this ecstasy, they do not create it. In the past, when women were afraid they were being used by men and wanted assurance that there was more to their relationship than sexual desire and gratification, they asked, "Do you love me?" We believe they were asking more than, "Is this sexual relationship an expression of romantic love?" Instead, we believe they were searching for a deeper meaning for their relationship than either sex or romantic love. In our society, lover relationships are believed to be the only ones in which men and women can have deep enduring relationships. It is our belief that the deepest love relationships are not sexual or romantic but personal. This deeper love is unrecognized in our culture and therefore often confused with romantic love.

Deep personal relationships between the sexes are difficult to cultivate in our society because relationships between the sexes are governed by an updated version of the world in which we grew up. Our world was really two worlds—the worlds of men and of women. Men didn't go into married women's houses unchaperoned. A woman's home was considered almost a sacred domain that men stayed out of except for the preacher or a trusted friend of the family. Boys played boys' games with boys and girls played girls' games with girls. Boys who played with girls or girls' games were called sissies or mama's boys; girls who played with boys and played boys' games were usually called tomboys. When girls played boys' games, it was assumed that they would play "like a girl." One girl who was raised in a family of boys did not learn to play like a girl. When a boy cheated in a neighborhood football game, she hauled off and slugged him and sent him home crying. This incident was reported to the author of the book, *Throwing Like a Girl* (Young 1990), as an example of a girl who not only didn't throw a ball like a girl, but didn't throw a punch like one. The author retorted, "Do you mean she threw a punch like a boy?" The storyteller responded, "No, she threw a punch like a boxer."

When boys and girls became young men and women, their primary relationship was that of potential lovers. When the relationship between a boy and a girl became serious, they were said to be "going steady." Then, according to local custom, passionate necking was permitted for good girls and for boys who had serious intentions. Girls who casually engaged in passionate petting or who "went all the way" when not engaged to be married were labeled as "bad girls." It was permissible for boys to use bad girls, but not good girls, for sexual gratification. The relationship between boys and girls was focused on love and sexuality. It was inconceivable that a close friend could be of the opposite sex.

In spite of our belief that we live in an enlightened age characterized by free relationships between the sexes, the tendency to place relationships between the sexes into either the category of "just" friends or "lovers" sounds strikingly like an updated version of the societal rules of our youth that were based on the primacy of sexual and love relations. Limiting relationships to "just" friends and lovers implies that the primary relationship between men and women should be that of potential or actual lovers.

Struggling with Cultural Misdirection

Most men and women recognize and develop their relationships in ways suggested by words that designate culturally preferred ways of being with the opposite sex. For this reason, they usually don't recognize their love as dialogical love when they experience it. They try to force their relationship into the "just" friends or lover categories. These are the only names they know to articulate relationships between men and women outside of courtship and marriage. Our interviewees all indicated that difficulty in naming had hindered the development of their relationship and that they had struggled to overcome that limitation.

"The word *love* is one example of that. Jeanne talks to me about the resonance, the engagement, the care that she feels for me. And I can say, 'Oh, yeah. I like that.' Which is a short version of the tension that we had to work through for a while on that. . . . I love Jeanne, but not in the sense that I have said that to other women in the past—where it became exclusive, objectified as a relationship that has certain kinds of boundaries. When we started to say to each other 'I love you,' we had lots of discussions around that because of the sense that now we are closing off a relationship. So that, 'I love you' in my past has been a disclosive statement but it has also been a way of saying, 'Now we know what the relationship is; it's not going to be ongoing; it's not going to be a process.'" (Russell)

Russell and Jean find that traditional interpretations of love inhibit rather than foster the development of their relationship. They found it difficult to speak of their love for each other because traditional love language meant a possessive limiting relationship. Their relationship requires a meaning of love that, as yet, has not been articulated.

How fulfilling relationships between the sexes can be inhibited by traditional labels is evident in *My Best Friend's Wedding* (1997). This movie concerns three relationships: Julieanne's friendship with Michael and with George and Michael's love relationship with Kim. Julieanne's friendship with Michael is the focal relationship of the movie. She is the best friend referred to in the title. Their friendship began in college and has continued for the past nine years. They have enjoyed sex with each other but not as an expression of romantic love. The love they share is akin to dialogical love. They understand each other in a way that comes from personal encounter and open sharing of hopes, values, and visions. Julieanne and Michael obviously love each other but they are not "in love." They accepted the dictates of our society that being "in love" is essential for marriage. Since they were not "in love," they decided not to marry but made a pact that when they became twenty-eight, if neither had found the "right person," they would marry each other. When Julieanne is on the verge of her twenty-eighth birthday, she receives a message on her answering machine from Michael to call him concerning an urgent personal matter. She assumes that he is calling to affirm their earlier agreement. Instead, she discovers that he wants her to support him in his marriage to a younger woman with whom he has fallen in love.

She goes to the wedding celebration to disrupt the marriage rather than support Michael's choice. The proposed marriage seems very fragile. The bride, Kim, lacks the strong personal relationship to the groom that Julieanne has. Further, it seems unlikely that Kim will develop a strong personal relationship with Michael. When their differences threaten their marriage, Kim persuades Michael to reaffirm their marriage by saying she is so in love with him that she will completely rearrange her life to suit his and that she will become whatever it takes to be his wife. When Julieanne recognizes that Michael is really "in love" with Kim, she shows her personal love for him by supporting the marriage.

During all the turmoil, Julieanne is supported by George, a homosexual who is her confidante, during her trials at the wedding celebration. He comes to the wedding festivities twice to support her, and she is constantly on the phone with him for advice and encouragement. In the final scenes of the movie, after Michael has left with his new bride, Julieanne and George celebrate with an ecstatic dance that discloses their personal love for each other. The climax of the celebration comes when George exclaims, "Maybe there won't be marriage and there won't be sex [with a grimace], but by God there will be dancing!" (*My Best Friend's Wedding* 1997).

JACK: When I saw the movie the first time, I had difficulty recognizing how well these two relationships illustrated the meaning of dialogical love. Much of the movie seemed to be a typical Hollywood comedy filled with connived shenanigans in which Julieanne attempts to disrupt the wedding. The movie supports the well-worn Hollywood theme that romantic love with the right woman conquers all. The "right" woman is an attractive, young, "bubbly" girl who seems to have nothing in common with her future husband except that they're "in love." The absence of personal love in their romantic love is made evident by the presence of Julieanne with whom Michael shares a deep personal love. That "romantic love wins out" over such a relationship so perturbed me that, at first, I failed to recognize that Julieanne personally loved George as well as Michael.

ANNE: I was appalled that Kim showed that she was the "right woman" by her willingness to make herself over completely to suit her husband-to-be. She gave up her education, her future career, a stable home life, and her personal way of being to satisfy Michael. In contrast, Julieanne was a strong woman whose bond with Michael came from her determination to be herself in her relationship with him. She seemed to be out of character when she played the part of an anxious woman whose fear of losing Michael led her into bizarre attempts to sabotage the wedding. When she confesses to Michael that she now recognizes that she was really "in love" with him all along, I was unconvinced. Her profession of romantic love seemed inauthentic when compared to her personal love for Michael.

JACK: Michael also loves her personally, but he is misdirected by a popular version of romantic love. I can't see how Julieanne and Michael, who often professed their opposition to traditional ways, could buy into the romantic view of love traditionally affirmed by our society and exaggerated by Hollywood. Without being blinded by romantic love, Michael would have dismissed Kim as an attractive "silly little girl" stuck in traditional values.

ANNE: Romantic love blinds us to personal love. Michael has obviously loved Julieanne for the whole nine years he has known her. From their relationship of dialogical love, he has developed appreciative love for Julieanne as a person. Tragically, he does not know that he loves her and that she really is the right person for him. From his limited point of view, he can be a friend to Julieanne but not a lover. To him, love and friendship are entirely different ways of being.

JACK: Do you think Julieanne's romantic idea of love and marriage prevented her from seeking to marry Michael during their nine years of friendship?

ANNE: Actually, she seemed to have disdain for traditional romantic love until she thought she would lose Michael to the "right woman." I believe that Julieanne did not seriously consider marriage until Michael decided to marry Kim because she valued her freedom.

JACK: In the sixties, many young people, like Julieanne, regarded individual freedom as an end in itself and marriage as a restraint on freedom. They believed that you should keep your sleeping bag rolled up behind the couch and form no relationships that in any way restricted your freedom. If that's your major concern, you are not apt to give yourself fully to relationships of dialogical personal love.

ANNE: I was searching for greater autonomy when we first met. But from being in our relationship of dialogical love, I've come to a new understanding of freedom that goes beyond freedom from restraint. I have become free to be more fully myself through being with you.

JACK: I had been a self-centered autonomous individual who, when we met, was in the process of discovering that personal relationships were worth the loss of some autonomy. We both have discovered that in a dialogical love relationship, you become more fully yourself than you could ever have imagined being. We found abundant being in a relationship of dialogical love rather than in a relationship that makes individual freedom an end in itself.

ANNE: Abundant being comes as grace when we courageously follow the possibilities that appear in relationships of dialogical personal love.

JACK: Courage is required because we do not know where we will be led by pursuing the possibilities offered us or what we will become by following them.

ANNE: When Julieanne and George are dancing at the end of the movie, they love each other in a way they never imagined possible. Their joyful ecstasy as they danced was not the ecstasy of traditional lovers. When George proclaims, "Maybe there won't be marriage and there won't be sex [with a grimace], but by God there will be dancing!" (*My Best Friend's Wedding*), I wanted to add, "The joyous ecstatic dancing of partners who love each other personally."

JACK: The ecstasy of their dance was like the ecstasy usually associated with romantic love. I was startled by such ecstasy early in our relationship. If I had been asked if that ecstasy came from love or friendship, I would have said friendship, but that did not adequately express what I felt about our relationship. I think we, like George and Julieanne, were experiencing what we now call dialogical love. Dialogical love is freeing because it does not limit experience to fit predeveloped categories. In dialogical love, you respond to the other person as he or she is present to you, directly and noncategorically.

ANNE: George does not relate to Julieanne primarily as a heterosexual woman but as Julieanne whom he loves. Julieanne loves George in the same way she loves Michael. She loved each of them personally. Her relationship with them differed only in that one could have led to Eros and marriage and the other could not. She delights in the presence of both of them, enjoys them ecstatically, lives in a common we-world with them, shares their joys and sorrows, and personally appreciates each of them. These are qualities of dialogical love relationships. Dialogical love is recognized by a qualitative way of being together, not by whether it includes or excludes sex or romantic love.

JACK: Julieanne obviously loves both men in the same dialogical personal way. In the case of Michael, his acceptance of the primacy of romantic love prevented him from recognizing their personal love, but in the case of George, it did not. Obviously, Michael and Julieanne loved each other but did not know it because their love was unrecognized.

ANNE: I would like to see a sequel to *My Best Friend's Wedding* that pursues how the best friends relate to each other now that Michael is married to Kim.

JACK: That sequel would have to deal with a problem that we and others we have interviewed have faced, namely, how do you have a close personal relationship with a person of the opposite sex when you are married to someone else.

ANNE: I think that the sequel would deal with a more difficult problem than the one we've had. Kim conformed to a traditional gendered way of relating to a husband when she gave up the life that she had planned in order to satisfy Michael and decided either to hide her real personality from him or to remake it in order to suit him and his lifestyle. Neither of our spouses have made such demands of us and, in fact, have in general supported our particular ways and aspirations. That's one reason we have been able to develop a strong personal relationship with each other and to continue our fulfilling way of being with our spouses. They both recognize that they cannot fulfill aspects of our being in the way that we can fulfill them together.

JACK: Just as they have supported our personal development, we have encouraged theirs.

ANNE: I wonder what would happen if Kim later decided to assert her own being by forming a personal relationship with a man who was more like her in style and aspirations than Michael? That would be an even more interesting sequel than how Michael and Julieanne could continue to develop the relationship they already have.

JACK: That sequel would concern how Kim's new relationship would foster abundant being not possible in her marriage.

ANNE: Rollo May points out that the primary reason for developing relationships between men and women outside of marriage is "not for sex per se but for relationship, intimacy, acceptance, and affirmation" (May 1969, 311).

JACK: None of those we interviewed gave desire for sex as the reason for forming relationships outside of marriage with persons of the opposite sex. Their reasons were overwhelmingly directed toward personal fulfillment through relationships they could not adequately articulate.

ANNE: Unlike them, Michael seems to have been searching for the right woman with whom to fall in love so that he could marry her. He seems to have the traditional view that his wife ought to give up her plans and aspirations in order to neatly fit into her husband's professional and personal plans. His romantic love for Kim is the opposite of dialogical love.

JACK: In contrast, Michael's friendship with Julianne fits dialogical love well. He delights in Julieanne's independent unwillingness to become someone else in order to be his friend. He loves and appreciates her as the person she is. Unfortunately, he doesn't recognize this relationship as love or that it could flourish in a marriage relationship. Julieanne only seems to want a romantic love relationship when faced with the prospect of losing Michael. But her celebration with George at the conclusion of the movie shows her delight at being free of the prospect of being "in love" in a marriage that would limit her personal way of being.

ANNE: For Julieanne, George is not a homosexual but a friend who loves her and whom she loves personally. Both of them seem to become fully aware of their personal love and acknowledge that love in their dance celebrating the freedom of dialogical love.

Must Sex Inhibit Friendship?

JACK: The imaginative relationship between Julieanne and George was described by partners in an actual gay-straight friendship when they affirmed, "We're not lovers, but we do love each other" (Whitney 1990, 115).

ANNE: Gay-straight friendships do not have to contend with the tensions that are often believed present when a love relationship is introduced into a friendship. That claim received popular attention when, in the film, *When Harry Met Sally* (1989), Harry says "men and women can't be friends—because the sex part always gets in the way."

JACK: Is it that sex and romance get in the way of friendship or that we have been taught that they are entirely different relationships that are mutually exclusive?

ANNE: A study at the University of Michigan challenged both beliefs by reporting that there was no difference in the quality of friendship between men and women that involved sexual relationships and those that did not (Elkins and Peterson 1993, 504). This study also concluded that men desired personal friendships as much as women do and that they develop fulfilling personal friendships with women as readily as women do with other women. But friendships between men and men in that study were found to be much less fulfilling than friendships between men and women and women and women (507).

JACK: In a more extensive study, Kathy Werking (1997) found that friendships between men and women are becoming more common but are not often studied. Werking concluded that "typically the friends were verbally and nonverbally affectionate with one another; hugging, kissing, linking arms, and saying, 'I love you' to one another" (94). Her study indicated that friends loved each other but in a different way than romantic love. One woman put it this way, "I just love him more than anything, so I guess that's it. Just that you can really love someone even if it's not like romantic love at all. Just love" (109). Werking observed that cross-sex friends "talked about what the word *love* meant in the context of their friendship. It is interesting to note that they had some difficulty expressing this in large part, I believe, because we are not linguistically equipped to describe platonic male-female love" (95).

ANNE: Platonic relationships in our society often merely mean an absence of sexual or romantic relationships. Is this what she means by platonic? Werking certainly stresses the difficulty cross-sex friends have in avoiding romantic sexual relationships. Oddly, she fails to consider those cross-sex friendships in her study that did include sex, as the Michigan study did.

JACK: Regardless of that significant omission, an important finding of Werking's study is that cross-sex friendship can be more highly valued than relationships based on sex and romance. One man asserted that "his future romantic partner would need to accept his cross-sex friendship" (Werking 1997, 151). One woman said, *"I will not marry anyone who does not accept my relationship with Alex"* (151). Another woman declared, "Men have come and gone in my life, you know, and Scott has always been there, . . . I would sacrifice any relationship that I had with a man for the friendship I have with him" (148).

ANNE: In those three relationships, cross-sex friendship is interpreted as personal love in which the partners enjoy, trust, and are committed to each other. All three of these relationships are similar to Julieanne's relationship with Michael. They love each other but they are not "in love." They seem to be saying, "I value this personal love friendship so much that even the person I fall in love with will have to accept this relationship as a condition of marriage."

JACK: Werking's study shows how much students value their love-friendship. It implies that in the future relationships such as ours will be more common and perhaps will find cultural recognition. It also indicates the need for further articulation of the differences between friendship and love and the place of dialogical love in relationships between the sexes.

Chapter 3

DIALOGICAL LOVE: FRIENDS OR LOVERS

"The word *love* is one example of that. Jeanne talks to me about the resonance, the engagement, the care that she feels for me. And I can say, 'Oh, yeah. I like that.' . . . I love Jeanne, but not in the sense that I have said that to other women in the past—where it became exclusive, objectified as a relationship that has certain kinds of boundaries." (Russell)

"Yeah, he's my boyfriend. And Bob is my best friend and Andy up there is like my soul mate. And like the three together is just wonderful! There's things about all of them [that I like]. And of all of them, I *could* live with Andy." (Sue)

ANNE: The preceding vignettes indicate that both Russell and Sue have found traditional views of love and marriage are too restrictive for abundant being. Russell and Jeanne had difficulty using the word *love* in their own relationship, because the word had a possessive quality that walled off their relationship. Sue divorced her husband in search of freedom but then felt free to claim him as her best friend and form other relationships that were needed for her abundant being.

JACK: What makes those two quests for abundant being especially interesting is that Russell is a member of a university community in an urban environment in another country, and Sue is a

35

waitress in the rural south. I'm glad we chanced on the interview with Sue. She gave us a perspective that those of us who live in university circles often miss. Academic language can unintentionally bias treatments of love and friendship in ways that subtly ignore the experience of people who do not share that vocabulary.

ANNE: Sue was an unusual and delightful waitress we met while on a professional trip. She volunteered to participate in one of our interviews when she discovered we were writing a book about relationships between men and women and especially relationships that were close personal ones that did not necessarily involve sex. She said she was involved in such a relationship, but it turned out that she was involved in three relationships, only one of which involved sex.

JACK: Actually, the relationship that she thought would be of interest to us turned out to be her former husband, who she called her best friend. Her second relationship, her boyfriend, was her friend and lover. Her third relationship, her soul mate Andy, was right on target. That relationship seemed to have qualities of dialogical love.

ANNE: Her best friend and boyfriend are examples of friendship and love as ordinary folks identify them. Her down-to-earth treatment of these relationships helped give us a different perspective from C. S. Lewis (1960) and Rollo May (1969), whose scholarly interpretations of Eros (love) and philia (friendship) inform the discussion of love and friendship in this chapter.

JACK: We selected Lewis and May as the focus of our discussion of love and friendship because they stress personal love in their treatments of the relationship between men and women. Lewis and May treat love and friendship within the context of the three loves—Eros, philia and agape—that have informed the consideration of love by many philosophers, theologians, and other scholars in this century. These three loves have been roughly distinguished from each other as Eros—the love of lovers for each other; philia—the love of friends for each other; and agape—the gracious love of God for humans often referred to by Jesus and Paul in the New Testament.

ANNE: Both Lewis and May show how the three loves of the Greeks can productively inform discussions of love and friendship. But I think we should begin with the relationship of sex to Eros. That's what most people expect when you say that you are going to treat love relationships between men and women. Sexual-romantic love is what most people mean when they say, "We are in love." By romantic love, they mean that love that you fall into that controls you, and I believe, leads to unwarranted expectations of your "wonderful" lover. By sexual love, they mean the desire for and the experience of sexual gratification.

Lewis on the Transformation of Sex by Eros

Lewis contends that when most people refer to the love they experience, they are talking about Eros. Eros, according to Lewis, is focused on the relationship between the partners and not on sexual gratification. He distinguishes Eros from sexuality by pointing out that sexuality is what we share with other animals while Eros is a human experience. He rejects the claim that Eros is primarily sexuality, contending that sexual experience can occur without Eros. He believes, however, that sexuality can be transformed by Eros into a human experience (Lewis 1960, 131–132). When a person is in love, according to Lewis, he or she is preoccupied with the beloved. In fact, he claims that the fact that "she is a woman is far less important than the fact that she is herself" (133). The lover primarily desires the beloved rather than sexual experience or sexual gratification. Lewis contends that when Eros takes over a person, the erotic reorganizes that person's world, including the meaning and importance of sexuality. "Eros wants the Beloved" whereas "Sexual desire, without Eros, wants *it*"—sexual pleasure (134).

When "a lustful man prowling the streets," says "that he 'wants a woman,'" he does not mean that literally; instead, "he wants a pleasure for which a woman happens to be the necessary piece of apparatus" (135). In contrast, in Eros a man desires neither a thing nor a woman but a particular woman. The "lover desires the Beloved herself not the pleasure she can give" (135). Eros transforms the need for sexual pleasure into a relationship with the beloved in which sexual pleasure becomes a by-product (136).

Lewis believes that in our time people take sex far too seriously. He contends that this somber seriousness has been promoted by the study of sexuality and the way sex is treated in the mass media (139). He points out that, in the past, people tended to make jokes about sex and see it as humorous. For them, sex was an ecstatic encounter to be playfully enjoyed, not a somber task to be undertaken as it is today. When sexual relationships are encompassed in a relationship of Eros, lovers can see the humor in sexual relationships. From the vantage point of an Eros relationship, Venus herself "is a mocking, mischievous spirit, far more elf than deity, and makes game of us" (141). Venus prompts lovers to exchange heated glances in situations in which they cannot openly express their erotic attraction for each other; then later in a situation in which a full encounter is possible, one of them finds it impossible to respond. Lewis says that in such situations those who have deified Eros experience the "resentments, self-pities, suspicions, wounded vanities and all the current chatter about 'frustration.' . . . But sensible lovers laugh. It is all part of the game; a game of catch-as-catch-can, and the escapes and tumbles and head-on collisions are to be treated as a romp" (142).

ANNE: I would have understood better what Lewis meant by saying Eros can transform sex into a human experience, if he had described more fully how this transformation takes place. He merely advises us not to take sex too seriously and to approach it playfully.

JACK: Certainly, he is right in contending that we take sex too seriously. Sexologists have contributed to long-faced preoccupation with sex. I can hear Dr. Ruth saying, "First, do you love each other? Well, that's nice. Now let's move to the crucial issue. Do you have orgasms? Have you tried . . ."

ANNE: Are you sure you are being fair to Dr. Ruth?

JACK: Probably not. I'm engaging in exaggerated caricature in order to make the point that in our society we do overstress sexuality, especially orgasms and the techniques for achieving them. Brief physiological pleasure has come to be more prized than a personal love relationship that transforms sex into a human experience.

ANNE: Why doesn't Lewis describe how that transformation occurs? Being playful may improve sex, but playfulness would improve sex for those who merely want pleasure as well as for those who want a personal relationship.

JACK: When I first read his contention that Eros makes sex human, I thought it questionable. Why human and not personal? Gilbert Meilaender (1978) helped me resolve that issue. He contends that Lewis believes that sexual appetite "needs to be personalized" by Eros "so that it becomes a part of something quite different—a truly human relationship between two persons in which each finds in the other the 'constant impact of something very close and intimate yet all the time unmistakably other, resistant—in a word, real'" (143). For some reason, Lewis prefers the word *human* to personal, but he is actually talking about desire for being with a particular person in a personal relationship. He says that "Eros makes a man really want, not a woman, but one particular woman. In some mysterious but quite indisputable fashion the lover desires the Beloved herself, not the pleasure she can give" (Lewis 1960, 135).

ANNE: I agree that some relationships are essentially mysterious and are incapable of description in the sense of describing a process. But I think the reason his failure to describe how sex is personalized results from his inadequate treatment of the lived body. He believes that bodies are something we have (143). For that reason, Lewis can contend that naked people simply become anonymous universal he's and she's and that people can only express their individuality by the way they dress (147). He is treating the body as an object to be looked at as opposed to the expressive body that is encountered in intimate personal or sexual relationships. Most people in an intimate embrace would experience the individuality of the other person more fully if he or she were naked than if he or she were clothed.

JACK: Lewis's inadequate treatment of the expressive body contrasts sharply with Simone de Beauvoir's erotic generosity, as interpreted by Debra Bergoffen (1997, 34–36). Erotic generosity refers to self-disclosure to another through the body as lived.

Self-disclosure comes not only from speaking but from bodily movement and from touching. This way of self-disclosure challenges the contention that disclosure comes only through rational use of language or from the clothing we select for others to look at. When I risk myself through open disclosure of myself to another, I experience ecstatic joy in our full mutual presence to each other.

ANNE: That's not difficult for me to grasp. After all, I'm a dancer and a nurse. I certainly know the meaning of disclosure through touch and bodily movement.

JACK: Lewis did write longingly of the day when men communicated with each other through touch (1960, 93). Somehow I find it hard to imagine Lewis disclosing himself through touch to a male or a female instead of doing it through speech and appearance.

ANNE: He did disclose himself to Joy through touch after they were married and Joy opened up a new world to him.

JACK: Beauvoir believed that you should generously disclose yourself to other persons and delight in their presence (Bergoffen 1997, 81–82). The living presence of those persons whom we choose to relate to personally are the source of our joy. Erotic generosity fosters the abundant being that we believe comes from being together in dialogical love.

ANNE: I wonder if in missing the significance of bodily disclosure Lewis doesn't miss what most people call love. He says that when people say they are in love, they generally mean love for the beloved and not sexual attraction. I suspect that most people mean by love passionate bodily disclosure to and with a beloved that is sexual but more than sexual.

JACK: Lewis names this more as Eros and makes it the context that transforms sexual relationships from animal appetite into human desire for a particular person, hence, making it a human experience.

ANNE: That's true, but I am not willing to let Lewis off the hook as easily as you and Meilaender do. I'm suspicious of exalting human experience over animal appetite. Animals do not abuse their mates sexually in the way that some men have abused the women I counsel. I think that abuse, in part, comes from thinking of the body as something you have. If a body is something you have, it is something you can use. Lewis claims that males use their bodies to dominate females and females use their bodies to be submissive (Lewis 1960, 145). But if a body is not something you have and your sexuality is something you are, then it is possible to engage in personal sexual relationships. You can share your being with another bodily, and they can respond bodily. In such an encounter, I would substitute giving and receiving for dominance and submissiveness. Giving is not an expression of maleness or receiving a female response. In this giving and receiving, who gives and who receives should depend on the persons and the situation not on their gender.

JACK: Had Lewis dealt with this kind of dialogical sexual relationship, rather than merely treating sexuality as an appetite to be transformed, his distinction between sexuality and Eros would have been less sharp. After all, personal sexual encounters are uniquely human experiences.

ANNE: Frankly, I don't know what it means to say that these unique personal encounters are transformed by Eros. I don't see what saying that sex has been transformed by Eros contributes to love relationships in which the expression of love is given personally in sexual encounter of lived bodies before the proclamation of, "I love you."

May on How Sex Is Transformed by Eros

May gives a more adequate description than Lewis of how sexual appetite is transformed by Eros into a personal relationship. For May (1969), like Lewis, Eros names a personal love relationship between men and women, whereas sex denotes a physiological drive. May points out that in our time Eros has lost much of its humanistic meaning. Erotic has become almost exclusively associated with sexuality and especially with sexual titillation (72). The function of sex is "the release of tension," whereas the function of Eros is to give "the spirit of life" to sexual relationships (73). Sex, defined physiologically, consists of "building up of bodily tensions and their release" (73); in contrast, Eros is experienced as personal intentions that give meaning to the sex act. "The end toward which sex points is gratification and relaxation, whereas Eros is a desiring, longing, a forever reaching out, seeking to expand" (73). Consequently, sex seeks closure in the release of tension, whereas Eros seeks to prolong excitement—"to hang on to it, to bask in it, and even to increase it" (73). Sex drives us from behind whereas Eros attracts us and draws us from ahead. The aim of sex is orgasm and the thrust of sex is to get on with it, to relieve the tension, to relax and rest. In contrast, the aim of Eros is union between persons that brings fulfillment. The thrust of Eros is to ecstatically enjoy being together, and hence Eros seeks to postpone and enhance, rather than terminate, the ecstasy. Afterward, rather than rest, Eros fosters thinking of the beloved, savoring the relationship, and discovering new facets of the experience together (74–75).

Although May focuses Eros on the relationship between men and women, he points out that Eros, as used by the Greeks and specifically by Plato, had a much broader meaning. "Eros . . . constitutes man's creative spirit. Eros is the drive which [sic] impels man not only toward union with another person in sexual or other forms of love, but incites in man the yearning for knowledge and drives him passionately to seek union with the truth. Through Eros, we not only become poets and inventors but also achieve ethical goodness" (78).

For May, love becomes personal when it moves from drive or need to desire. Drive and need are physiological urges that push us from behind, whereas desire "pulls us ahead to new possibilities" (310). "If love were merely a *need*, it would not become personal. . . . Choices and other aspects of self-conscious freedom would not enter the picture. One would just fulfill the needs. But when sexual love becomes *desire*, . . . one chooses the woman, is aware of the act of love, and how it gets fulfillment is a matter of increasing importance. . . . For human beings, the most powerful need is not for sex per se but for relationship, intimacy, acceptance, and affirmation" (310–311).

ANNE: May certainly does describe more fully than Lewis how Eros transforms sex into a human way of being together, even though he does it from a male perspective. He gives a wonderful description of how sexuality is transformed by erotic desire. His descriptions are moving and convincing. May's description of the relation of Eros and sex helps me better understand how erotic desire can transform sex in the way Lewis claims that it does. But a greater issue for me than transforming the animal into the human concerns how impersonal human relationships are transformed into personal ones. I wish they had discussed how to transform impersonal human sex into personal sexual relationships.

JACK: That would interpret sex in a way that is appropriate to dialogical love relationships. Dialogical love is a personal relationship in which culturally imposed distinctions between male and female have no ordering power, as such. In dialogical love, two persons are directly present to each other and that aspect of their presence that is usually attributed to sex or gender is primarily experienced as personal presence.

ANNE: One person we interviewed described sexual encounters in a way that showed how sexual relationships can be personal.

"My past sexual relationships were very different from my relationship with Helen. In the past, the sex act seemed basically the same no matter who my partner was. Of course, different partners varied in skill, body movement, thoughtfulness, aggressiveness, and the rest, but except for that, the sex act was similar. My sexual relationship with Helen is profoundly personal. I feel the presence of Helen in every movement. The ecstasy we experience is not so much from sexual turn-on as from personally being together sexually." (Tony)

JACK: As I remember it, Tony humorously commented that their being personally present to each other was so ecstatic that orgasms were often experienced as an anticlimax. Their relationship seems to me to show how sex would be experienced in relationships of dialogical love.

ANNE: But that should not blind us to the worth of Lewis's and May's interpretations of Eros. By treating sexual erotic relationships as personal ones, they come closer to dialogical love than most treatments of Eros I've read.

JACK: Actually, May and Lewis have similar interpretations of Eros. But when they consider friendship, they give opposite interpretations.

Lewis on Friendship and Eros

Unlike May, who defines friendship as a face-to-face relationship, Lewis treats friendship as a side-by-side relationship and contrasts it with the face-to-face relationship of Eros. Lewis makes such a sharp distinction between Eros and friendship that they become radically different ways of being with each other.

Lewis contends that persons become friends when they discover they share the same truth and choose to engage in common pursuits. He quotes Emerson with approval when Emerson says, as Lewis interprets him, "*Do you love me?* means *Do you see the same truth?*" (Lewis 1960, 97). Lewis contends that without such common pursuits and concerns, there "would be nothing for Friendship to be *about;* and Friendship must be about something" (98).

In contending that friendship has to be about something, Lewis does not mean that friendship is valuable because of the uses that can be made of it. In fact, he believes that friendship has its own inherent worth and value. He contends that friendship does not consist of the good acts that friends do for each other, such as becoming our ally, caring for us when we are sick, standing with us in the face of our enemies, and caring for our widows and orphans. These "good offices are not the stuff of Friendship" (102). Friendship comes from common concerns and pursuits and has its own worth.

The common pursuit of truth is so much the focus of friends, according to Lewis, that friends are uninterested in each other's personality except as it relates to the pursuit of the truth. Friends don't want to know about their friends' pasts, jobs, connections, or any other personal matters. Lewis believes that when friends are absorbed in a common quest or vision, that vision and quest becomes "the very medium in which their mutual love and knowledge exist" (104). If we attend to the friend and not to what friendship is about, "we should not have come to know or love him so well" (104). Lewis believes that engaging in common quests develops an appreciative love that is at the heart of friendship.

Lewis contends that in our society people overvalue love relationships and undervalue friendships. He thinks that most people have lost the ability to recognize friendship as a legitimate love. In contrast to the contemporary focus on love and sex, Lewis points out that to "the Ancients, Friendship seemed the happiest and most fully human of all loves" (87). In contrast to Eros, which is emotive, friendships are "luminous, tranquil, rational" (89) relationships that are freely chosen. Lewis finds it strange that the modern world has no interpretation of friendship that would elevate it to the level of love or that would interpret it as love. He contends that tears, kisses, and embraces that were commonly shared among males in the ancient world are not only missing from the modern world but are actually forbidden (93).

Lewis observes that it is possible to have "erotic love and friendship for the same person yet in some ways nothing is less like a Friendship than a love affair" (91). Lovers always talk about their love; friends hardly ever talk about their friendship. "Lovers are normally face to face, absorbed in each other; Friends, side by side, absorbed in some common interest" (91). Unlike Eros, friendship does not inquire about another's affairs or past. Friendship is interested in the pursuit of the same truth. Unlike Eros, the love of friendship "ignores not only our physical bodies but that whole embodiment which consists of our family, job, past and connections. . . . Eros will have naked bodies; Friendship naked personalities" (103).

Since Lewis believes that friendship comes out of common pursuits, it follows that men and women will rarely be friends in societies in which they live very different lives. "Where men are educated and women not, where one sex works and the other is idle, or where they do totally different work, they will usually have nothing to be Friends about" (105). Lewis admits that in vocations such as college teaching, the possibility of friendship between men and women exists, threatened only by the possibility of erotic disruptions. When persons of different sexes discover common concerns, interests, and pursuits, according to Lewis, "the friendship which arises between them will very easily pass—

may pass in the first half an hour—into erotic love" (98). Erotic love introduces an alien force into friendship because erotic love is compulsive and obsessive, unlike friendship. Since the presence of women disrupts friendship, Lewis laments the invasion of women into men's circles.

ANNE: Lewis's interpretation of friendship is certainly a one-sided masculine one. The "good old boys" at Oxford are engaging in common intellectual pursuits that are disrupted by emotional and erotic women. Frankly, I'm fed up with men blaming women for sexual attraction that lures them away from their projects.

JACK: I agree! But I also disagree with Lewis's contention that sexual attraction inhibits close friendship between the sexes. I know he often overstates his position, but even allowing for that, he seems to rule out lasting friendships between men and women who are erotically attracted to each other.

ANNE: He certainly does when he tells his readers how to cultivate the appreciative love that characterizes friendship. To experience appreciative love you need to stand side-by-side with a person and "fight beside him, read with him, argue with him, pray with him," rather than face him and gaze "in his eyes as if he were your mistress" (104). Statements like that infuriate me.

JACK: How can Lewis appreciate his friend engaged in their common pursuit if he does not face him? Their relationship would have to be at least half-faced, in that he would have to face the friend engaged in the common task to appreciate him. It seems to me that appreciative love comes from facing your partner when engaged in common pursuit.

ANNE: Appreciative love also develops in face-to-face friendship of dialogical love. When you face your friend, you appreciate his or her way of being with you. May's interpretation of friendship captures this way of being a friend.

May on Friendship and Eros

May focuses friendship on being present to each other rather than on the shared pursuit of truth, as Lewis does. According to May, friendship "accepts the other's being as being; it is simply liking to be with the other, liking to rest with the other, liking the rhythm of the walk, the voice, the whole being of the other. . . . Philia does not require that we do anything for the beloved except accept him, be with him, and enjoy him" (May 1969, 317). Friends accept each other and learn to accept that acceptance. Friendship, in contrast to Eros, does not come "from a drive from behind or an attraction from in front, but emerges silently from simply being together" (317–318).

May believes that Eros "cannot live without philia" because the tension produced by the continuous attraction and passion of Eros would be unbearable if it did not relax. "Philia is the relaxation in the presence of the beloved" that "gives a width to Eros; it gives it time to grow; time to sink its roots down deeper" (317). The unhurried time required by friendship runs counter to the hectic pace of today's living; thus, the potential contribution friendship can make to our lives is often lost in our time. Friendship is not only important for its own sake, but through friendship, according to May, we develop our sense of identity (319).

ANNE: May's interpretation of friendship comes much closer to what I mean by friendship than Lewis's. I think most women would find May's view of friendship much more acceptable. Men tend to think of friendship as doing something together, whereas, we women tend to think of friendship as enjoying each other.

JACK: Well, I'm a man, and I would define friendship more as May does than as Lewis does, if I had to choose between them. But it's possible to have both kinds of friends. I have friends that fit Lewis's definition of friendship in that we like to think and argue together in pursuing the truth. I also have friends with whom I like to play tennis and fish. I would call this kind of friendship a side-by-side friendship, but I would not call such a relation friendship merely on the grounds that we enjoyed doing the same things together. A friend of mine who is a real serious tennis player once said he would play tennis with the devil if he gave him a good game. I don't think he would call the devil a friend just because he enjoyed playing tennis with him and admired the way he played. Friendship implies that you enjoy the person as well as the game, or better, that you enjoy the person while both of you are engrossed in the game.

ANNE: Most of the time you and I enjoy what we are thinking about and each other in that thinking. Although it is possible to distinguish side-by-side relationships from face-to-face ones, in relationships of dialogical love, such separation seems artificial.

JACK: I believe that May would reject that artificial separation, but he seems to me to have created another artificial separation of human experience. I find his contention strange that friendship contributes relaxation to face-to-face erotic relationships, especially since he interprets friendship so personally. May seems to limit ecstasy to erotic relationships. I wonder what he would think of my having felt ecstasy as intense as that of lovers that seemed to come from our friendship. Prior to that experience, like May, I had associated ecstasy with Eros but not with friendship. What I once thought came from friendship, I now believe comes from dialogical love that, as May says of friendship, emerges "silently from simply being together" (318).

ANNE: When dialogical love silently emerges from being together, the distinction between friendship and love becomes less clear. Lewis and May both show how love as sexual attraction can become personal love, but their treatment of friendship as personal love is less adequate for our purposes. Lewis fails to show clearly how friendship is a personal love and May fails to show adequately how friendship can be distinguished from love. On the few occasions when they treat the possibility of friendship between men and women, they do so briefly and in passing by contrasting friendship with Eros. We need to consider the possibility of friendship between men and women more fully.

Chapter 4

FRIENDSHIP BETWEEN MEN AND WOMEN

JACK: All of the people we interviewed, if they had to designate their relationship as a friend or lover, would choose friendship. But the experience of their relationship is too special to be designated as friendship in the conventional sense. This specialness is somehow related to its being a friendship between a man and a woman, but why this is so is unclear. We need to consider treatments of friendship that are specifically concerned with relationships between men and women, such as those given by Caroline Simon and Robert Solomon.

ANNE: Simon, a feminist, treats intergender friendship specifically and far more extensively than either Lewis or May (Simon 1997b, 145–175). Like Lewis, she regards love as a threat to friendship, but she believes that developing intergender friendships are worth the risk (Simon 1997a).

JACK: She helped me see Lewis's interpretation of friendship in a different light. She quotes Lewis: "The typical expression of opening Friendship would be something like, 'What? You too? I thought I was the only one.'" She points out that this recognition of common concern can apply to many different matters. In such friendships, friends become loved "as unique, irreplaceable individuals" (Simon 1997b, 101). I had originally interpreted Lewis to mean that friendships were formed by people

49

pursuing common truth and that friends were valued primarily as fellow seekers of that truth.

ANNE: Reading Simon's book helped me to recognize the difficulty that we have encountered in treating what she calls intergender friendship. Most love relationships are treated as relationships between men and women and most friendships are treated as relationships between men and men and women and women. Simon goes beyond the usual approach by devoting a chapter to friendship, another to love, and then one to intergender friendship.

Simon on Intergender Friendship

Simon contends that intergender friendship is a species of general friendship (Simon 1997b, 152). She gives a succinct definition of general friendship: "Friendship . . . is based on endorsing a person's vision of himself or herself as relatively fitting to his or her destiny and committing oneself to helping the friend attain that vision" (102). Friends encourage and support each other in their pursuit of their own particular destiny. She does believe, however, that "as my care for my friend leads me to love what he or she loves," it is possible for "my friends' plans and projects [to] become my own." For this reason, in "loving my friend, myself expands and is enriched by his or her accomplishments and delights" (102). Thus friendship contributes to our personal growth but that is not its end. "The aim of friendship is befriending: encouraging and helping others in fulfilling their conceptions of their destinies" (104).

Friends can help friends achieve their destiny by helping them gain insight into the meaning of their destiny. Helping a friend in this way requires a delicate balance that attempts to "speak the truth in love with concern" but ensures that the friend will write and live his own story in the achievement of his or her destiny (105). Learning how to speak to a friend in this balanced way "is learned though careful reflection on lived experience" (106).

Friendship is different from love as Simon interprets it. According to Simon, romantic love is based on the idealized attraction for men as men or women as women that aims at union. This inclination toward union is fulfilled in marital love, in which partners share a common destiny. This tendency toward union with shared destiny leads couples to experience their relationship as a *we*. Simon concludes that "marriage is the appropriate institutional manifestation of *we*" (123). For Simon, sexual fidelity and permanence are essential qualities of the martial *we*, but she points out that that *we* involves much more—"sharing a mortgage, sharing a bank account, and sharing a bed . . . and the responsibilities of parenthood" (124). Although shared common destiny is the fundamental stress of marriage, Simon acknowledges that marriage needs to make room for each partner to fulfill his or her particular destiny. Marriage involves a dialectical tension between the destiny of the *we* and the destinies of you and me.

In contrast to marital love, intergender friendship stresses the fulfillment of the particular destiny of each partner more than a *we* destiny. Simon is unclear concerning how far this goes. She does claim (Simon 1997b, 125), as Nozick does (1989, 82), that a person can only be involved in one *we* relationship in which personal identity is involved.

According to Simon, both marital love and intergender friendship love involve tension between union with shared identity and autonomy with individual fulfillment. In both of these loves, the tension needs to be in balance. "As romantic love moves toward martial love, the fulcrum that strikes a creative balance within love's dialectic is not at the center, but toward the side of union. In intergender friendship, the fulcrum is far farther toward the side of individuation" (Simon 1997b, 152). This creative balance is attained in intergender friendship when friends contribute to each other's destiny without "allowing any existing sexual undertones to impel them toward union" (152). Simon believes that achieving this creative balance is possible for men and women who are married but not to each other only when they are committed to upholding marriage vows. This commitment makes it possible for these men and women to be friends "without trying to be asexual" or "pretending to be genderless" (Simon 1997a, 189).

ANNE: Simon claims that her treatment of intergender friendship tests "Meilaender's hunch that 'friendship between the sexes may take us not out of ourselves but beyond ourselves and may make us more whole, balanced and sane than we could otherwise be'" (147). Do you think that her treatment does?

JACK: Simon ignores the context in which Meilaender envisions those possible contributions of intergender friendship. He sets the context for those possibilities in J. B. Priestley's treatment of the possibility of men and women really talking with each other. The first condition for such talk, according to Priestley, is that "sex must be relegated to the background. . . . The man and woman must be present as individualities, any difference between them being strictly personal and not a sexual difference. They will then discover, if they did not know it before, how alike the sexes are" (Priestley 1926, 57, quoted in Meilaender 1994, 192). Second, when men and women are "'secure in this discovery' of how alike they are, . . . they will discover how unalike the sexes are. Third, when they bring their differences together in dialogue, there will be another kind of 'talk between the sexes, the dual and duet of impersonal and personal interests, making in the end for balance and sanity and in the progress of the talk, adding to its piquancy'" (Priestley 63ff., quoted in Meilaender 1994, 193). It's in that context that Meilaender states his hope that "friendship between the sexes may take us not out of ourselves but beyond ourselves and may make us more whole, balanced, and sane than we could otherwise be" (Meilaender 1994, 193).

ANNE: It's encouraging that in the 1920s Priestley had such an insight. Today there is more communication between men and women, but even so, real dialogical openness between the sexes is rare.

JACK: In relating to each other, we've discovered that relationships between the sexes can lead us beyond ourselves and make us more balanced and sane. However, I wonder if it is sound to attribute that to the difference between the sexes, as Priestley does. When I first encountered Simon's intergender friendship, I thought, "Now there's a term we can use!" We had found it awkward to say "persons who are married but not to each other." That designation also omits men and women who are not married but are close personal friends. Intergender friendships seem to cover them. But the term "intergender friendship" is inadequate for relationships such as ours because these friendships are personal relationships that are not gender-based.

ANNE: That's why I applauded when Priestley advised persons of different sexes to forget about sex differences and concentrate on being individuals. I would have liked it better had he said, "be persons" rather than individuals. I think men and women are more alike than different, and further I think that personal differences are far greater than gender differences, whatever they may be.

JACK: It is difficult to discern what gender differences actually are. Our contention that sex is physical and gender cultural is a clear distinction, but it omits the possibility of psychological or spiritual differences between men and women that are neither primarily physical nor cultural.

ANNE: That's *the* issue! I don't think we'll ever know the answer to that question until we get rid of all the garbage and that won't occur in our lifetime. By garbage, I mean those cultural gender differences that clearly have to do with power relationships that are left over from times in which men had to fight and hunt and women cared for children and home. I mean such garbage as women are naturally subservient, that men can't care as women do, women are emotional and men are rational, and on and on and on.

JACK: There is a practical way of getting rid of the garbage. I discovered it in arguing with colleagues concerning differences in the races when we were integrating the schools. I asked them if knowing that a student was black would tell them how that particular student should be educated. Of course, they admitted that it would not. I think we could say the same thing about women and men. A practical way of dismissing much of the garbage is acknowledging that there is no predictable individual difference between men and women other than physical ones.

ANNE: Neither is there any predictable sexual attraction between particular men and women or between particular men and men or women and women, in homosexual relationships.

JACK: Simon's term, intergender friendship, obviously doesn't cut it, but what do you think of her treatment of friendship and love as *we* destiny in the case of marriage and individual destiny in the case of friendship?

ANNE: It seems obvious to me that a married couple share a *we* destiny as long as they remain in a marriage relationship. But I don't see why friends can't have such *we* destinies. We obviously do, and our *we* destiny makes possible the abundant being we share.

JACK: Yes, but our *we* destiny has come at a high price. We chose our destiny, but Bobby and Mary did not choose to be involved in our *we* destiny. They are involved because they chose marital *we* destinies with each of us. They seem to recognize that our personal fulfillment is involved in the *we* relationship that you and I share. I'm amazed that they support us in the way that they do.

ANNE: That's why this book is dedicated to them. I think that Simon and Nozick oversimplify *we* relationships. They contend that if you enter into another *we* relationship, it is because you are seeking a better one, and that shows that your former *we* relationship is over (Nozick 1989, 78; Simon 1997b, 124). They seem not to recognize that *different* *we* relationships can be formed to foster ways of being not possible in the original *we* relationship.

JACK: Mary recognized that she could not fully foster my particular destiny early in our relationship. When I asked her to marry me, she responded that she did not think she could share in that aspect of my being that sent my thought soaring out of the everyday world. When I responded that I wanted a lover, a wife, and a family, we were married. I highly prize our *we* relationship of marriage and family. The *we* relationship that you and I share in no way indicates that I am seeking a better *we* relationship than Mary and I share, only a different one.

ANNE: The same is true of me. Your soaring off in thought is what first attracted me to you and eventually led to our *we*. At first I found it both thrilling and frightening, but over the years it has led to a *we* identity. Without that identity, I can't imagine being the person I am now.

JACK: I remember how frightened you were when that was taking place. You had just made a speech to a women's group admonishing them to abandon the hen's nest and soar like eagles. You turned to me one day and said, "When you're soaring and look down, it's sometimes terrifying."

ANNE: I recognized how my identity and destiny were involved in our *we* relationship. Here we were soaring together with no community support and facing uncertainty that those in *we* relationships of marriage do not encounter.

JACK: The relationship that we were developing was so new to us that we had difficulty articulating it, much less finding an acceptable place for it in our culture. Now after sharing a long *we* destiny, we finally have articulated our relationship as dialogical love. Do you think that defining love relationships, friendships, and intergender friendships primarily in terms of destiny contributes to the articulation of our relationship?

ANNE: Doesn't that depend on how destiny is defined?

JACK: Simon defines destiny as "a range of possibilities that should be brought to fruition but which a person can choose not to cultivate. Destinies are inherently both goal-oriented and normative" (Simon 1997b, 16). She contends that the primary task of our destiny is to become "our true selves" (16).

ANNE: Our *we* relationship has led us to become more our true selves, but so has our *we* relationship with Bobby and Mary. Our relationship with them is different from our *we* relationship with each other. But doesn't love and friendship involve more than destiny? For example, Simon fails to grasp the interactive mutual quality of friendship. That became evident to me when I read the fictional description of the friendship that Simon chose to disclose the true meaning of friendship. In that friendship between Charity and Sally (Stegner 1987), Charity did foster Sally's individual destiny, but Charity was so rule-governed and dominating that it was virtually impossible for her to share in a mutual interactive relationship with Sally. While I believe that I should foster my friend's destiny, that hardly seems an adequate definition of the essence of friendship.

JACK: How do you friend me? Let me count the ways. You call me to be *we,* your laughter lights our way, the unassuming way you handle tasks with dispatch and good humor moves us on, your free spirit encourages us to soar, your grasp of possibilities transforms gray times into vibrant happenings alive with color, your touch draws me from my reflective mind into my lived body. I'm just getting started, and could go on and on before I added your being in our destiny and your sharing in my destiny.

ANNE: Our readers may think that your purpose is to compliment me. In your own way, you do. But in what you have just said, I recognize your backhanded way of saying that while destiny is important in love and friendship, it does not distinguish friendship from love as clearly as Simon thinks and that there is much more to love and friendship than destiny.

JACK: Yes, and I believe that Solomon's treatment of friendship between the sexes and its relationship to love will make that evident.

Solomon on the Complementary Relationship of Friendship and Love

Robert Solomon (1988) defines friendship more like May does than either Lewis or Simon. He treats friendship as a face-to-face personal relationship rather than as a side-by-side relationship that pursues common endeavors or fosters each other's destiny. "Friendship is loyal, caring, trusting, wishing the other well. Friendship also involves intimacy, and inspiration, and the sense that one's life is not complete without the other" (315).

Like May, he believes that there is a complementary relationship between love and friendship. "Friendship is not always love, and love is not necessarily friendship, but they complement and reinforce one another. . . . Is friendship essential to love? No, but it is essential to love's lasting for it is the foundation of love" (315). He feels so strongly about the relationship between love and friendship that he asserts that "if love doesn't turn into friendship, that might just mean that it wasn't love" (316). He says "sexual desire and satisfaction don't *mean* anything without friendship" (315). His treatment of friendship as foundational focuses on the inequality of love relationships and on the equality (316). He contends that if there's no friendship in a love the inequality will eventually lead the love relationship to fall apa. says, "Unlike love, friendship always assures as well as demands equality, and so becomes the ideal model and foundation for love" (316).

The demand for autonomy, as well as for equality, is another way that friendship differs from love, according to Solomon. He says that the "tension in love between possession and respect for the other's autonomy and freedom is soothed in friendship, for in friendship, unlike love, there is little possessiveness and the other's autonomy and freedom are in no way a threat or a danger" (316–317).

Solomon contends that the reason for possessiveness in love relationships is that lovers identify themselves with the other in a way that is usually not true of friendship. That is because the "essence of love . . . is precisely the formation of self, a shared self . . . and self-identity" (Solomon 1981, 301). He contends that in the private "love world" of "mutual support . . . maximization of self-esteem can indeed be astounding" (302–303). He does recognize that in the case of "inseparable friends" or romantic friendships, this sense of identity also may be present, but not as fully as it is in love that has "exclusive and all-or-nothing features." In contrast, "friendship—with sex or without—raises fewer expectations, is more tolerant and easygoing than the most open romantic relationships" (Solomon 1988, 318).

He gives an excellent example of a personal love friendship between a man and a woman:

———

"Two friends of mine—who are inseparable friends of *each other*—have spent the past six or seven years together and are as intimate and as happy as any romantic couple. One of the activities they seem to enjoy most together—or at any rate spend the most time doing together—is lamenting their individual difficulties in finding a decent lover, someone they can trust and get along with as well as get excited about. All of us—their friends—have made the obvious suggestion: that they have just this already, and why don't they just get it together and stop their whining. But though they love each other, find each other extremely attractive and in fact have spent years of time together, and despite the fact that they have both found every other relationship in their recent history to be disastrous (to put it mildly), they continue to insist that they do not love one another 'in that way.' They know each other too well, they explain; they think of one another as brother and sister. They are both romantically hungry, even while enjoying a most delectable friendship." (Solomon 1988, 319–320)

———

ANNE: That relationship is similar to the relationship of Julieanne and Michael in *My Best Friend's Wedding* (1997). In our earlier discussion of that relationship, we indicated a possible reason for this couple's inability to conceive of each other as potential lovers. They seem to believe that "falling in love" is a better basis for marriage than a deep personal love for each other.

JACK: Solomon contends that we look for different characteristics in friends than in lovers. In friendship we look for "loyalty, intelligence, our shared interest . . . and more personality than looks," whereas in a lover we are attracted by "a certain sexual charm, a set of fantasies, more looks than personality" (Solomon 1988, 322).

ANNE: If love is characterized by sexual charm, fantasy, and looks, no wonder Solomon believes that it won't last. It's also clear why he believes that love needs to be founded on "loyalty, intelligence, shared interest and personality," characteristics of friendship.

JACK: Solomon seems to believe, with Aristotle, that the highest form of love is friendship when friendship is at its highest level. The highest level of friendship moves beyond utility and mutual enjoyment to the third level of friendship that, according to Aristotle, is a friendship of mutual virtue—that is, two friends who are mutually inspiring and "bring out the best in each other" (Solomon 1988, 317). At this level, Solomon claims that the distinction between friendship and love loses its meaning. In spite of Solomon's many criticisms of May for being a Platonist, I find much similarity in their treatments of friendship and its relationship to love. Both believe that friendship is necessary to complement and complete love. Both believe that love has a higher level of being that discloses what love really is. In fact, Solomon defines Aristotle's highest level of friendship as real love and contrasts it with romantic love and contends that, at the highest level, love is indistinguishable from friendship (317). He also contends that the perfect friendship of Aristotle "is the friendship celebrated by the speakers at Plato's *Symposium*" (Solomon 1981, 12). The Greeks are very different from we moderns who tend to sharply distinguish friendship from love and confine deep personal relationships to love relationships. Solomon wonders "why we are so adamant about distinguishing friendship from romantic love, that is, apart from the initially obvious fact that the latter is intrinsically sexual and the former is not" (Solomon 1981, 10). Solomon points out that "love in the West doesn't come so neatly packaged" as interpreting love as Eros, agape, and philia imply (10).

ANNE: Solomon raises an issue that has concerned me since we began interpreting our relationship. Does dredging up the Greek terms for love (agape, Eros, and philia) confuse or help us understand the meaning of personal love relationships?

JACK: I plead guilty to thinking about our relationship in that context. Aside from its being the intellectual context in which I learned to think about personal relations, it seems a more adequate way to think about love relationships than the tendency in our culture to use love to mean everything from love of pecan pie to the most exalted personal relationship. You and I have used those distinctions in trying to interpret our relationship to others, but we both know that they are inadequate. In fact, at one time, we thought we needed a fourth Greek term to describe our relationship.

ANNE: And then, do we need other Greek terms for every relationship that doesn't fit into the traditional Greek categories but is not like ours?

JACK: The problem is not the terms but the categorical way in which we use them. We use terms to confine as well as define relationships.

Instead of using terms to limit our experience, terms can direct us to general ways of relating to each other that we recognize from our own experience. Terms used directionally can help others recognize the type of relationship meant as well as suggest relationships that can be experienced. Then the term *friendship* could point to deep fulfilling personal relationships that are love relationships as the Greeks interpreted them and that Lewis longed to have restored in our time.

ANNE: That's characteristic of what we have called dialogical love. That leads to a startling conclusion, at least for me, that maybe the Greeks had it right! I think we should consider the difference between Plato and Aristotle on love and friendship, but I have misgivings about doing so. Such considerations often lead you philosophers to get bogged down into technical philosophical scholarship and excessive criticism that almost inevitably leads us away from the theme we are pursuing.

Plato and Aristotle on Friendship

Gilbert Meilaender (1981) begins his study of friendship with Plato and Aristotle because they "offer us representative expressions of what may be the two most important competing theories of friendship. For Plato, friendship is a universal love which grows out of more particular, affective attachments. For Aristotle . . . it is a narrowing down of the many toward whom we have good will to a few friends whom we especially choose" (8).

We choose our friends for three reasons, according to Aristotle. The first is that they are useful to us. The second is that we enjoy being with them, and the third and highest is that they inspire us to be virtuous and to foster virtue for its own sake. In contrast, Plato believes that friendship moves from mutual attraction to a higher level of friendship, being drawn into that level by the vision of ideal beauty and goodness. Interestingly, the source of this interpretation of friendship is a woman, Diotima. In contrast to Plato, it's inconceivable that mere women would be a source of wisdom for Aristotle. Aristotle believes that we choose friends whose virtues and visions are similar to ours. Plato believes we choose friends whose virtues complement ours, but we recognize their virtues as good ones that we don't possess adequately. Aristotle believes that the highest good is happiness and that happiness comes from self-realization. Friends help us realize our best self and thus contribute to our happiness. Plato believes that happiness comes as a gift from the pursuit of the good and beautiful (*Symposium* 1961, 204d–205a, 210–212; *Nicomachean Ethics* 1941, 1155–1157:35, 1171a).

ANNE: Let's keep focused by considering what Plato and Aristotle can contribute to the quest for the meaning of dialogical love. Considering the difference between our and their society and culture, can they speak to our concern about deep love relationships between men and women?

JACK: First of all, the Greeks were male chauvinists par excellence. Athens was a community of male citizens and those outside of the citizenry were outsiders, and this was especially true of women. Most Athenian citizens and especially Aristotle would never have considered the possibility of friendship between men and women. Aristotle is talking about choosing a few friends from a wider circle of male friends. You choose as close friends those with whom you have like virtues and interests and who would foster your virtue.

ANNE: The friendship proposed by Aristotle presupposes a society of close association of males like that of Athens. Close associations of that sort don't exist between men and women in our time or in any time that I know of. I certainly didn't have a wide circle of male friends from which to choose you!

JACK: But didn't you select me because of my virtues and the likelihood that I would foster your virtue?

ANNE: I'm surprised by the implication of your flippant remark! I've always thought of you as more of a Platonist than as an Aristotelian.

JACK: I'd rather not be known as either. Such identification often leads to placing people in philosophical schools and then attacking the school. Frankly, I think Solomon does that to May when he accuses him of being a Platonist and then attacks Platonism rather than May's specific treatment of love. As I said earlier, I'm amazed at how similar their positions on love and friendship are when the labels are dropped. Then Solomon's valid contention that May includes too much in Eros can direct us to a productive focusing on Eros as passion for other persons and for personal relationships. These passions are like the Greek passions in that they are called forth by recognizing the worth of someone or something. Thus, as May puts it, passion calls us into being from encountering worth beyond ourselves, rather than from appetites pushing us from behind. Passion is not experienced as a need to be met nor as an obsession. It is experienced as desiring to be in personal relationships with others through which we become more than we are.

ANNE: Passion in May's sense, whether it's Platonic or not, is certainly what we and those we studied have experienced. That passion draws us ahead toward the abundant being that comes into being when we are *being* together.

JACK: Our passion is initially for abundant being, but then it becomes passion for the other person as you recognize his or her worth. Although you appreciate what your partner's way of being contributes to your abundant being, your passion for him or her comes from recognition of the worth of that person quite apart from what he or she contributes to you.

ANNE: You also passionately affirm what you become from being together. In addition, you passionately affirm your relationship or, as we prefer to put it, the way we *be's* together.

JACK: In summary, our passion is for abundant being, each other, our way of being, and for our selves as we are called into being.

ANNE: That raises an issue that bothers me. It sounds to me like we are saying we want abundant being and that to get it, we form friendships.

JACK: Do you mean that we make abundant being our goal and regard friendship as a means to achieving that end? Philosophers quarrel over whether Aristotle viewed friendship as a means of achieving self-realization that leads to happiness and over whether Plato views particular friendships as a means of gaining vision into the good and beautiful. I think both interpretations fail to do justice to each philosopher's view of friendship because they assume a modern form of egoism developed by modern psychology that I'm not sure is present in either Plato's or Aristotle's thought.

ANNE: May attacks that egoistic approach when he contends that Eros relationships do not originate in appetitive needs that push you from behind, but from recognizing possibilities that draw you ahead into fulfilling relationships.

JACK: But if we use Plato, as May did, to question the soundness of needs psychology, we would consider how personal relationships are transformed by visions of the good and the beautiful. We need to focus on how relationships of dialogical love questions needs psychology. George Kunz (1998) helps by showing how being called into being by other persons challenges needs psychology. Kunz contends that needs psychology is an egocentrism that informs much of contemporary psychology. "The *psyche* of modern psychology is the *ego* establishing itself in the center of the individual personality, constructing its own identity, manipulating its environment to feed its needs, and enjoying the pleasure of satisfying those needs" (10). Kunz challenges the *egology* of contemporary psychology by proposing *psukhology*. "This *psukhology* is the study of the self's having its identity inspired by others, animated by others, empowered by others" and especially by responding to the weakness of others by accepting "responsibility *to-and-for-others*" (11).

ANNE: As a nurse, I like Kunz's contention that we are called into relationships of responsible care for those who need our care. He contends that egocentric psychology is one-sided, in that it cannot account for responsible care in the way that psukhology can.

JACK: We share with Kunz the conviction that persons are called into being by others in personal relationships. But Kunz puts more stress on persons coming into being by accepting moral responsibility to care for those in need than on personal encounter that engenders abundant being as we have done. I think that Kunz could expand his psukhology by including personal love relationships in it. Our work as well as Kunz's suggests that the human sciences need to be rethought in our time to take into account how persons are called into being by others.

ANNE: That's true, but it raises the question we still haven't dealt with adequately. Is pursuing abundant being through personal relationships a high-level form of egocentrism? That would make friendship a means of pursuing abundant being rather than satisfying needs. A psychology of egology would make friendship one means, among others, for achieving happiness. From this perspective, happiness can be achieved directly. This brings us back to the question, can happiness, fulfillment, or as we put it, abundant being, be achieved by forming a friendship?

JACK: Personal relationships like ours foster abundant being, but that abundant being cannot be pursued directly by forming a relationship as a means to an end. Abundant being comes as grace to those who forget their needs and enter into relationships of dialogical love with their whole being.

ANNE: Not only that, but the abundant being fostered by dialogical love relationships is recognized as morally good, as we attempted to show in chapter 2. At least in our case, it has led us into helping create, establish, and maintain a free clinic and to interpret nursing in a way that stresses the moral sense of nursing care. Good work is called forth by dialogical love in a different way than from striving to achieve moral goodness as an end. The partners are called into good work by their experience of abundant being. That good is integrally involved in abundant being in a way that defies willful pursuit of moral goodness.

JACK: I can't imagine either of us thinking that we ought to continue our friendship because it will make us better persons or accomplish morally good works. Our friendship does, in fact, do that, but our passion for our relationship and for each other does not seem to come from pursuit of the good, as Plato says, or from our desire to be virtuous, as Aristotle contends.

ANNE: We have dealt with the issue of whether happiness or goodness can be pursued directly by forming a friendship, but we have not dealt with another issue in Plato and Aristotle's treatment of friendship. Plato favored complementary virtues and Aristotle like virtues in friendship.

JACK: It seems to me that any friendship and love relationship would involve both complementary and similar virtues and talents. Complementary relationships seem to foster joint pursuits and projects, as we are experiencing now in the writing of this book, and as we both experienced in our relationships with Mary and Bobby when we were young married couples building careers, forming families, and raising children. Our dialogical relationship seems to spring more from being alike in what we enjoy and pursue than from complementary differences.

ANNE: Friends and lovers are involved in both complementary and like relationships. Perhaps the reason Sue needed three different friendships with men was that each relationship was limited to one way of being. One of Sue's enduring friendships was a complementary relationship and the other was a relationship of similar kind.

JACK: Her relationship with her best friend (former husband) was one in which they brought complementary skills and spirit together to engage in common tasks. Their relationship, however, involved more than pursuing common projects. As Sue put it, "He was always there for me." Solomon, May, Simon, and Lewis do not seem to adequately recognize that being there for each other is essential to friendship.

ANNE: Sue and her soul mate were very much alike. They simply enjoyed being with each other. They would spend all night engaged in interesting and intimate conversation: a way of relating that her former husband (now best friend) found uninteresting. When she was with her soul mate, they would sleep together. Here sleeping really meant sleeping that was interrupted only by good conversation rather than sex.

JACK: Their relationship was one of dialogical love, in that their ecstasy emerged from a personal relationship rather than from sexual or romantic roots. The ecstasy comes from being in the presence of a particular person. That person is not experienced as "my man" or "my woman" but as this particular person I love.

ANNE: Sue's lover relationship was the least enduring of her three relationships. She developed a friendship that eventually expanded to include sex. She said the sex was nice but confessed that if she had to choose a partner to live with, it would be her soul mate not her lover. Obviously, she felt she could get along without sex but not without deep personal relationships. In that respect, I'm very much like Sue. I've always thought that sex was something I could take or leave. By that I don't mean that I'm uninterested in sex or don't think that it's important, but I don't order my life around sexual relationships. Like Sue, I don't think that sex should be the defining element in relationships between men and women. When relationships between men and women are primarily personal, they should be developed in many ways depending on the persons and their situation. Sexual relationships are one possible way, but I can't see why they should define the relationship.

JACK: Sue included sex in a face-to-face friendship that was not an Eros relationship. The possibility of a personal sexual relationship in a friendship would be difficult for Lewis or Simon to entertain. But Solomon points out, "that one can have sex with a friend—even magnificent sex—without that relationship crossing over into romantic love" (Solomon 1988, 321). Solomon does, however, admit that introducing sex into a friendship can lead to complications. It certainly did in Sue's relationship with Tom. Tom wanted to marry Sue, but she would have none of it because she highly valued her freedom. Eventually, that ended their relationship.

ANNE: Sue said that if she got married, it would not be to her lover, but to her soul mate, Andy. It is interesting that both Sue's complementary relationship and her like relationship were the lasting ones. Why should we favor one over the other as Plato and Aristotle contend?

JACK: Plato and Aristotle differ more from us moderns than they do from each other. For example, they regard friendship as a higher relationship than Eros relationships. They do not make the sharp distinction between friendship and love that moderns make, nor do they confine intimate personal relationship to Eros relationships, as moderns do.

ANNE: Confining ecstatic deep personal relations to lover relationships greatly limits personal relationships. In saying that, I am not depreciating the importance of ecstasy in lover relationships. I am glad that lovers learn to expect and find ecstasy in love relationships. The fulfillment of that expectation shows them that ecstatic personal relationships are possible. But why confine ecstasy to one kind of personal relationship? Wouldn't it be wonderful if we were prepared to accept the ecstasy that can silently emerge from all personal relationships?

JACK: It would! But can you imagine Lewis rewriting *The Four Loves* to include ecstasy in each one and revising his treatment of Eros and friendship to show how alike they are at the highest level? Even with his sharp distinction between friendship and love, however, I must credit him with recognizing, with all the difficulties involved, that men and women can be real friends. There is a wonderful line in the play, *Shadowlands* (Nicholson 1989), that concerns the friendship between Jack (as Lewis was called by those close to him) and Joy. A friend comments to Lewis, "You know how people talk." Lewis retorts, "I don't know and I don't care. A like-minded man and woman are entitled to be friends, it seems to me. I don't see why I should disqualify half the human race just because they're also available for other purposes" (45).

ANNE: "Available for other purposes!" Why does Lewis talk like that? I know that this expression was given to him by the author of the play, but in his writings he often says something that I am ready to affirm with a resounding "Amen," and then he ruins it with a comment that reeks of male chauvinism.

JACK: Perhaps we are not giving Lewis enough credit for struggling to overcome his male chauvinism. Before he met Joy, he ignored personal relationships between men and women as beneath the concerns of a learned man. In fact, Chad Walsh points out that, before writing *The Four Loves,* Lewis had merely treated love by concentrating "on the legalities of sexual love—confine it to marriage, otherwise be chaste" (Walsh 1976, 145). From that limited concern with Eros to his treatment of it in *The Four Loves* is an amazing transformation no doubt brought about by his relationship with Joy. We, of all people, ought to be aware of the difficulty of facing the tremendous changes that are taking place in the relationship between the sexes in our time. Perhaps we should abandon the whole male-female orientation and simply talk about ways of being together—side-by-side and face-to-face, complementary and like relationships, and personal and impersonal relationships.

ANNE: That's an interesting possibility, but shouldn't we also eliminate the tendency to limit personal relationships to friendship and love relationships? Why not merely say that dialogical love can transform and enrich our lives with abundant being without trying to force it into either friendship or eros categories?

JACK: But love and friend relationships are well established in our culture and dialogical love is not. As May says, love takes place within "the forms of the society." But he also contends that traditional forms are proving inadequate and that our generation is called to search for new forms. "In our transitional age, we are hunting, exploring, reaching about, struggling to assert whatever we can find in the experiment for some new forms" (May 1969, 320). One new form that some men and women are reaching for is the one we call dialogical love.

Chapter 5

REACHING FOR
DIALOGICAL LOVE

Lewis Surprised by Joy

ANNE: It is inconceivable that Lewis was reaching out for dialogical love before he was surprised by Joy.

JACK: Your play on words may be missed by those of our readers who aren't familiar with Lewis's life. He entitled his autobiography, *Surprised by Joy* (Lewis 1955), before he met Joy. He selected that title because his conversion to theism and Christianity was affected by his experience of being surprised by joy. His final surprise by joy actually was surprise by Joy. This surprise, as Chad Walsh (1976) points out, led him to a more human understanding of Christianity. His love of Joy and facing her suffering and death led him to question some of his former beliefs. He described the travail that tested his faith and made it concrete in *A Grief Observed* (Lewis, 1976).

ANNE: I think he was thrust out of the confines of the academy by his friendship and later marriage to Joy. As Chad Walsh (1976) pointed out, Lewis's relationship with Joy initiated the interests that led him to write *The Four Loves* (Lewis, 1960), which Joy edited for him.

JACK: But he reinterpreted his treatment of love and friendship in *The Four Loves* in his later book, *A Grief Observed* (Lewis, 1976), in which he considered the meaning of living through the suffering and death of Joy.

Lewis seemed not to have Eros or marriage in mind when he first met Joy. He was literally "surprised by Joy" as Walsh (1976, 136), his close personal friend, pointed out. Their relationship began when Joy corresponded with Lewis after her conversion from being a secular Jew to a Christian. Lewis was struck by the way that Joy's wit could "cut away" intellectual nonsense. In her, he found a worthy match "in the thrust and parry of debate" (138). After an extended correspondence, they finally met in 1952. A "warm friendship, based in part on strong and mutual respect, began to flower" (139). At that time, Joy was in the process of separating from her husband. When she discovered that her husband was in love with another woman, she returned to the States and was granted a divorce and the custody of her two sons. She returned to England in 1954 and resumed her friendship with Lewis. A year or so later, when Chad Walsh and his wife visited Lewis and had a chance to observe Jack and Joy together, his wife declared, "I smell marriage in the air." Walsh commented that "whether Lewis smelled it is more doubtful" (140). When they were married in April 1956, in a civil ceremony, Lewis described the marriage as a "practical formality" rather than a real marriage. Jack married Joy simply to prevent her deportation from England. At that time Joy was in ill health and only later discovered that she had terminal cancer. Joy's limited prospects for life became evident when the cancer shattered her thigh bone. Jack then married Joy in a religious ceremony in March 1957, and they lived together until her death in July 1960.

Their brief married life together was enhanced by an unexpected remission of her cancer. Then Lewis, "the expert on miracles, experienced one before his own eyes," Walsh observed (141). During the miraculous remission, Joy wrote the Walshes, "Jack and I are managing to be surprisingly happy considering the circumstances; you'd think we were a honeymoon couple in our early twenties, rather than our middle-aged selves" (141). Other letters spoke of her happiness and "celebrated Lewis's prowess as a lover" (142). During this time, Walsh observed that Joy "flowered as a woman—and a human being. It was, I think, an extraordinarily happy and buoyant marriage, though the shadow hovered always in the background" (143).

Lewis, who had turned away from erotic love as a young man, finally experienced firsthand "what sexual love between a man and woman can be at its best" (145). This new experience so forcefully informed *The Four Loves* that when it was delivered as lectures under church auspices, it aroused the ire of some of the clerics. These clerics had applauded Lewis's limited early writings on sexual love in which he contended that sex was to be confined to marriage, that the unmarried should be chaste, and that divorce was unacceptable for Christians. But his relationship to Joy changed all of this. He wrote to a friend, after what he described as a belated honeymoon, that he "never expected to have, in my sixties, the happiness that passed me by in my twenties" (146–147). Joy's remission ended in her death in 1960. Lewis experienced severe grief, and his own kidney and heart ailments took his life three years later.

After Lewis's death, Walsh wondered if Lewis "had been granted an additional ten years of good health, what might he have written? *Till We Have Faces, The Four Loves,* and *A Grief Observed* provide the clues. It was Joy that made them possible" (150). According to Walsh, *Till We Have Faces* was Lewis's most successful novel as a work of literature. In that work, "Lewis achieved a depth of human insight that excelled anything else he wrote, and pointed toward a talent for fiction that might have put him with the major novelists, if time and health had permitted him to continue" (144).

Although Lewis had experienced affection, friendship, and charity before Joy, his relationship with Joy made it possible for him to give Eros a convincing and powerful treatment. According to Walsh, Joy and Jack "learned from each other the mysteries of Friendship, Affection, Agape, and Eros at a depth that makes them kin to the great lovers found in literature and sometimes in life" (151). In *A Grief Observed,* Lewis "reveals the price paid for that knowledge" (151). Joy's suffering and death led him to question the goodness of God that he had so long championed. But Lewis moved from bitter attacks on God to a recovered, but tested, faith. Walsh observed that "in this most harrowing of his books, there is found also the radiance of a love that death itself could not dim. Lewis was indeed surprised by Joy—into his own self-knowledge and deepest fulfillment" (151).

ANNE: Your old professor Chad Walsh certainly gave a moving account of the relationship between Lewis and Joy or I should say Jack and Joy, as they called each other. I felt myself drawn into their story as he tells it.

JACK: Well, he was a good friend of Lewis's, and Lewis's writing greatly influenced his life. In fact, he was just finishing his first book on Lewis when I was in his class.

ANNE: I'm sure that his close friendship with the Lewises is why I was so moved by his description of their relationship. A first-person treatment of a story draws you into events of the relationship more than a third-person account.

JACK: I was moved much more by Walsh's description of the relationship between Jack and Joy than I was by Lyle Dorsett's account (1993). However, Dorsett's account is well worth reading. I read it nonstop after hearing his lecture on the relationship of Jack and Joy and our lively discussion afterward.

ANNE: But you were primed for it. As I remember it, we had just finished writing the story of Jack and Joy, following Chad Walsh, when we heard Dorsett's lecture. Later when I read Dorsett's book, I didn't think it added anything essential to the account of their relationship we had written drawing on Walsh.

JACK: No, it didn't, but that's not because Dorsett's account isn't well done. But Walsh's account is not only compelling, it treats all the essential events in their relationship. My recommendation to those who find the story of Jack and Joy as fascinating as we did is to read them both!

ANNE: But, as I remember it, you were a little troubled by Dorsett's treatment.

JACK: Yes, I was troubled by his tendency to interpret their relationship as a traditional courtship leading up to marriage. Jack and Joy seemed to me to have moved over time from a friendship into a dialogical love relationship.

ANNE: Walsh certainly did not treat their relationship as courtship moving toward marriage. He simply and movingly describes their relationship as he knew it as a close friend and confidante without trying to fit it into a category. Interestingly, both Walsh and Dorsett come to the same conclusion that in the end Jack and Joy became great lovers.

JACK: But what kind of love? Traditional love or what we have called dialogical love?

ANNE: Dorsett believes that Joy "dreamed of marrying" Jack early in their relationship. He gives as evidence that Joy told her friend, Bel, that "the most wonderful ecstasy came from just holding hands and walking on the heather" (Dorsett 1993, 112).

JACK: I recall similar ecstasy when we were together as friends walking on the heather in Sweden with your husband close at hand. Now we would attribute that ecstasy to dialogical love but not to the traditional "being in love."

ANNE: Walsh's moving account of their relationship prepares you for their eventual love relationship in marriage that breaks the bounds of gender.

JACK: Walsh's unfolding of their relationship encompassed much more than a traditional love story. The beautiful way he told their story often moved us to tears.

ANNE: I'm glad you said moved "us" to tears. I want our readers to know that you are often moved to tears more quickly than I am. I've had enough of comments that associate tears with so-called sentimental females. Such arbitrary gender distinctions are meaningless in the relationship we call dialogical love.

JACK: That meaninglessness is evident in what Lewis says of Joy after her death. "She was my daughter and my mother, my pupil and my teacher, my subject and my sovereign; and always, holding all these in solution, my trusty comrade, friend, shipmate, fellow-soldier. My mistress; but at the same time all that any man friend (and I have good ones) has ever been to me. Perhaps more. If we had never fallen in love we should have none the less been always together, and created a scandal. That's what I meant when I once praised her for her 'masculine virtues.' But she soon put a stop to that by asking how I'd like to be praised for my feminine ones" (Lewis 1976, 55–56).

ANNE: Listen to how Lewis responds to Joy's challenge. "It is arrogance in us to call frankness, fairness, and chivalry 'masculine' when we see them in a woman; it is arrogance in them, to describe a man's sensitiveness or tact or tenderness as 'feminine.' But also what poor, warped fragments of humanity most mere men and mere women must be to make the implications of that arrogance plausible" (57–58).

JACK: What an amazing confession for a man whose writing often contains that same arrogance. That this amazing transformation came from his reinterpretation of love and friendship is evident in how his statement, "If we had never fallen in love we should have none the less been always together" (56), sets the stage for his praising Joy for her masculine virtues.

ANNE: But the context for that transformation was his remembrance of how Joy retorted by asking how he would like to be praised for his feminine virtues. His response to Joy's challenge is to confess that arrogance leads us to call certain virtues masculine and others feminine. Isn't it arrogant when you call me "Manny Annie?"

JACK: I call you "Manny Annie" because some of your virtues and ways of being that I most value are labeled masculine by our society. When I speak of "Manny Annie," I am making fun of our culture and praising you for being honest enough to be yourself.

ANNE: How will we overcome societal gender biases if we continue to perpetuate the division of masculine and feminine, even in jest?

JACK: You did not respond to my jest as Joy did to Lewis's by asking me how I would like to be praised for my feminine virtues.

ANNE: I knew you would say, "Thanks for the compliment!" But why do we have to categorize virtues as masculine or feminine? Why can't they just be virtues that make a person admirable and lovable?

JACK: I don't know how we will change societal usage, but I do know that in dialogical love relationships gender designations make no sense.

ANNE: I think Lewis came to believe that, but he often does not express it well. Perhaps that's because he often uses traditional designations in trying to articulate groundbreaking relationships. His description of his relationship to Joy in that moving passage that sets the context for his rejection of the masculine-feminine distinction challenges his former distinction between friendship and Eros. His love of Joy encompasses "daughter," "mother," "pupil," "teacher," "subject," "sovereign," "trusty comrade," "friend," "shipmate," "fellow-soldier," and "mistress." In that amazing tribute to Joy, the distinction between the face-to-face of Eros and the side-by-side of friendship vanishes.

JACK: That's what we contend happens in dialogical love. Traditional love stresses sexual and gender difference. In dialogical love there are only personal differences that appear in dialogical relationships. Consequently, there is no "Manny Annie," only Authentic Anne.

ANNE: If Lewis had had more time to work through his interpretation of friendship and love, I wonder what effect it would have had on his Christianity.

JACK: One effect, we have already noted. Treating sexual relationships solely as what doctrine dictates as permissible or possible is no longer tenable for Lewis. From his experience of love, he contended that the Divine self-giving love called agape is directly encountered in Eros relationships (Lewis 1960, 184).

ANNE: I think that's true. I was appalled when you told me that some theologians had contrasted agape with Eros by contending that Eros was always self-centered. Lewis certainly rejects that interpretation.

JACK: An atheist, according to Lewis, could give the same self-giving care for those he or she loves that a Christian could, and would be encountering the same God in that self-giving love. The main difference between them, according to Lewis, is that the Christian will praise God for the gift of love. Lewis affirms that "when you are happy, so happy that you have no sense of needing Him, so happy that you are tempted to feel His claims upon you as an interruption, if you remember yourself and turn to Him with gratitude and praise, you will be—or so it feels—welcomed with open arms" (Lewis 1976, 4). Jack's relationship with Joy certainly helped him recognize that Divine love is present in natural love.

ANNE: Their relationship also led him in the direction of affirming dialogical love. He certainly valued its stress on the concrete presence of the other. He said that the "earthly beloved . . . incessantly triumphs over your mere idea of her. And you want her to; you want her with all her resistances, all her faults, all her unexpectedness. That is, in her foursquare and independent reality" (77).

JACK: It seems to me that being with Joy in life and death brought Lewis into the concrete world that most of us encounter daily. I am suspicious when Christian faith does not interact with the concrete world. When I first read Lewis, he seemed, to me, to be stuck in a traditional faith unsobered by concrete encounter with the world. Joy made him face the concrete world of love, suffering, and death. In the concrete world, persons get old and face loss of powers as well as death. Is what we call dialogical love a relationship that is more appropriate for older, mature people than young persons? Plato contended that wisdom is possible only after fifty when, so to speak, the sap is no longer rising. Perhaps dialogical love relationships are better suited to those who no longer have to contend with the rising sap.

ANNE: Speak for yourself! When we first met, you were over fifty, but I was still in my early forties. Seriously, I think that in relationships of dialogical love, age and age differences are insignificant. Most of the couples we interviewed for this study were under fifty.

JACK: I rarely ever think of either of us in terms of age. Actually, there was a greater age difference between Jack and Joy than between us. They seemed to pay no more attention to age difference than we do. Joy thought of Jack as the same age as herself when she wrote of "our middle-aged selves" (Walsh, 1976, 141).

ANNE: A relationship that begins as a personal one rather than a sexual one will place less emphasis on age. Jack and Joy were first friends and only later lovers. Some of those we interviewed followed that pattern. Interestingly, they all believed that way was preferable to beginning as lovers and becoming friends when the sap subsides.

JACK: Solomon contends that love without friendship will not last. Lewis would seem to support Solomon's contention when he states that he and Joy would have remained together forever as friends had they not become lovers. However, that statement indicates a change in his view of friendship and an end to his former contention that love and friendship are radically different.

ANNE: When he rejected virtues as gender determined, he had moved far beyond his male interpretation of friendship as the good old boys pursuing truth together and his former radical distinction between friendship and love. Had he lived longer, I think he would have articulated love and friendship as integral expressions of the personal love he and Joy obviously shared.

JACK: It's possible that, although Jack's love for Joy united Eros and friendship, his language had not caught up to his way of being with her. Traces of his male chauvinist way of speaking and his previous separation of Eros and friendship are occasionally present in his articulation of their relationship. But his lived relationship with Joy and his reflection on its meaning was changing his way of thinking and speaking about it right up until his death. We well know how such experience and reflection can change the meaning of love and friend relationships. In fact, ours is still changing after more than twenty years. This book could not have been written without our continuous reflection on our we relationship.

ANNE: Goodness knows we've struggled to articulate our relationship. In contrast to our over twenty years, Jack and Joy's relationship lasted only eight years. Considering all that was involved in those eight years, I am amazed at how well they articulated the meaning of their relationship. Given more time, I believe that Lewis would have articulated their relationship in a way that would be clearly recognized as a dialogical love relationship.

Emerson's Rejection of Fuller's Invitation to Dialogical Love

Margaret Fuller reached out for a relationship of dialogical love with Ralph Waldo Emerson. He not only rejected her invitation to seek a new way of being together, he did not even understand what she was proposing. It is odd that Emerson was unable to understand the kind of friendship Fuller was proposing. They were friends and also leaders in American letters and thought in the nineteenth century. They belonged to the same circle of friends and scholars. Emerson was the center of that group, and Fuller was as much a full participant as a woman could be in that time.

They engaged in an ongoing argument concerning the nature of friendship in general and specifically of their relationship (Berkson 1988, 3–30). Certainly, they considered themselves to be friends, but their disagreement concerning the meaning of friendship raises the question of what kind of friends. Although there is no substantial evidence that they were lovers, some scholars have speculated that they were lovers and others that Fuller wanted a lover relationship but was rejected by Emerson. We are concerned with this dispute only as it relates to the difference in Emerson and Fuller's interpretations of the meaning of friendship.

The differences in their interpretation of friendship, according to Berkson, "represent two opposing modes of thought about issues of individualism, responsibility, intimacy, and the appropriate response to weakness and evil in human nature" (12). Emerson was the apostle of American individualism and self-reliance and interpreted friendship within this context (12). According to Emerson, friends should be chosen to foster personal growth. Friends perfect themselves by drawing on the imagination, intelligence, and wisdom of their friends. The function of friendship is to stir the imagination and intellect so as to foster the best in a friend. Friends should ennoble and inspire. Friends focus only on what is excellent and uplifting in their relationship (13). Fuller recognized the self-centeredness in Emerson's interpretation of friendship. She says that Emerson "weighs and balances, buys and sells you and himself all the time" (Fuller 1983, 2:161). Unlike Emerson, whose interpretation of friendship was based on contributing to the perfection of each other, Fuller believed that friends love each other even when they are suffering or failing (Berkson, 14–15). In Fuller's interpretation, friends care for each other, whereas in Emerson's interpretation, friends perfect each other (15). Fuller did believe, however, that friends improve each other, but they do so by seeking out and encouraging the potential of their friends.

Emerson's view of friendship was extremely individualistic. In his essay on friendship, he says, "I do then with my friends as I do with my books. I would have them where I can find them, but I seldom use them. . . . Though I prize my friends, I cannot afford to talk with them and study their visions, lest I lose my own" (Emerson 1941, 202). For Emerson, friends are there to stimulate your imagination and thought by sharing their ideas, insights, and perfections. Since their purpose is to stimulate your own thought, you do not need to understand their thoughts for their own worth or entertain their visions. Whereas Emerson feels his identity threatened by intimate friendship, Fuller feels her identity being lost by the absence of intimate friendship. Fuller often felt that she was not understood. "I feel quite lost; . . .To see so many acquaintances, to talk so many words, and never tell my mind completely on any subject—to say so many things which do not seem called out, makes me feel strangely vague and movable" (Fuller, 1:178). Fuller longed to "bring back the dear talking times of Greece and Rome" (1:189). She developed a program for women in Boston in 1839 in which she required the participants in that program to engage in dialogue and not merely listen to others and especially not to her. Significantly, when she invited Emerson to share in the conversation, he gave a lecture (Berkson, 20).

Since Emerson wanted to associate with people in order to develop and expound his own position, he only wanted to relate to those who directly supported and enhanced the development of his thought. In contrast, Fuller wanted to encounter a full spectrum of different thought to challenge and stimulate her thought. To her, friends were valued as much for their difference from her thought as for their support of it. Since Emerson only wanted to listen to thought that was congenial to his, he did not seriously consider Fuller's criticism of his interpretation of friendship for its lack of interaction, intimacy, difference, weakness, and hurt.

Emerson confessed that he could not understand Fuller. It seemed to him that they were "born & bred in different nations" (Emerson 1939, 353). It is clear, however, that Fuller understood Emerson. Fuller found it necessary to understand the men's world as well as her own; whereas, Emerson, like most men, needed only to understand the men's world. Emerson was the spokesperson for the idea of self-reliance that was sweeping male-dominated America. In contrast, Fuller was the spokesperson for what later became feminist philosophy at a time when most people were both vehemently opposed to her ideas and to a learned woman who would stand up and argue with men with intellectual rigor (Berkson, 22).

Fuller wanted a relationship with Emerson similar to the one we have called dialogical love. She wanted an intimate relationship that included real dialogue that took seriously what both partners believed and envisioned. She also wanted an interactive testing of each other's beliefs and values rather than the uncontested admiration of each other's thought that Emerson seemed to desire. For her, intimacy did not preclude honest differences squarely faced and tested in a critical dialogue. In contrast, Emerson seemed to believe that friends only admired and supported each other's beliefs in ways that boosted their egos.

Although Fuller wanted more rigorous testing of ideas by friends than Emerson did, she also believed that true friendship ought to be a relationship of intimacy and warmth. This is probably the reason that some people have claimed that she wanted a sexual relationship with Emerson. These interpreters seem unable to conceive of a love relationship of intimacy and warmth between men and women that does not involve sexual relations. Fuller desired a personal relationship with Emerson that could not be defined by the presence or absence of sexual relations. It is difficult, however, for those who are overly concerned about sexual relations, either positively or negatively, to seriously consider a personal love relationship, because they define all intimate relationships between men and women in terms of sexuality.

ANNE: Margaret Fuller really did try to expand Emerson's view of friendship. I really admire that woman for challenging such an eminent intellectual.

JACK: I'm not sure that he really recognized the challenge. It's safe to say that he didn't understand her search for dialogical love. After commenting that it seems that "we had been born & bred in two different nations," he goes on to say, "You say you understand me wholly. You cannot communicate yourself to me. I hear your words sometimes but remain a stranger to your state of mind" (Emerson 1939, 353). He complains that "sometimes you appeal to sympathies that I have not" (352). He advises her to, "Speak to me of everything but myself & I will endeavor to make an intelligible reply" (353). Apparently, he does not want to enter into a relationship that requires self-examination and -awareness.

ANNE: Not only does he not want dialogue that focuses on the self, he does not want to discuss his relationship with Fuller. He desires a "robust & total understanding [that] grows up resembling nothing so much as the relation of brothers who are intimate and perfect friends without ever having spoken of the fact. . . . It may do for others but it is not for me to bring the relation to speech" (352).

JACK: Emerson wants a friendship in which the partners never speak personally of each other, of themselves, or of their relationship with each other. No wonder he said that their "constitution" and "rhetoric" were so different that they seemed to have "been born & bred in different nations" (353).

ANNE: Unlike Emerson, Fuller was groping for an intimate relationship of dialogical love in which partners engage in dialogue and speak openly of each other, themselves, and their relationship. Unfortunately, no one seemed to hear her. It's difficult enough to get a hearing when your views are clearly developed and defined but opposed to what most people believe. But when you are groping to articulate a relationship that you would like to bring into being, getting a hearing often seems impossible. I hope our groping for dialogical love will get a hearing.

JACK: What I admired about Fuller is her persistent attempt to articulate the meaning of rich loving friendships between men and women.

ANNE: She must have been greatly discouraged when her attempt to develop an intimate and dialogical friendship with Emerson was misinterpreted as an attempt by a spurned unmarried woman to form a lover relationship with a famous man.

JACK: Misunderstanding of what you're about leads to incredible loneliness. I wonder whether Emerson and others recognized Fuller's loneliness. Loneliness can easily be missed when a person has many relationships and accomplishments that incline others to say how fortunate and fulfilled he or she must be.

ANNE: I wonder how much our loneliness fostered our quest for dialogical love.

JACK: Most people would be surprised to discover how lonely you have been. After all, you had twice won the highest award given nurses by the Virginia Nurses' Association and you were involved in almost all the worthwhile nursing endeavors in our community. As far as I can tell, you are admired and well-liked. You are a more likable, amenable person than I am. Perhaps more important, you seem to fit in and take part in the conversation of most groups.

ANNE: I think women that are personally or socially successful often appear less lonely than they are. Much of our lives revolve around everyday practical activities and attempting to adjust to community demands. We often are unable to talk with anyone about what matters in life. Talking about what is most important in life is the kind of dialogue you revel in, but you don't enjoy talking about or being involved in everyday practical matters. No wonder you are lonely.

JACK: I sometimes have wondered if the reputation I have for enjoying children hasn't come in part from being totally disinterested in what most adults talk about.

ANNE: Your loneliness doesn't just come from that. I remember when we first met, how strange and incomprehensible I found the world that you seemed to live in. Now, I find myself living in that "weird world." That's not because I have wholly adopted your world; you have helped me see the world in a different way. My basic values haven't changed all that much, but I came to recognize that some of them didn't fit well into the traditional world I inherited. Before we met, that incoherence frustrated me, but I didn't know why.

JACK: Trying to make sense of our lives and our world over the past twenty years has created the common we-world that we live in.

ANNE: That sounds more comfortable than it is. Our we-world requires us to keep reaching out to understand and articulate our relationship and the world in which we live.

JACK: But we haven't been able to fully comprehend or articulate either. Our relationship continues to change and evoke unpredictable responses from each other and especially from others.

ANNE: When we met, we were ready for each other. We were both very lonely, both reaching out for more, both convinced that the traditional ways would not lead us to that more, and both willing to take risks to find that more together.

JACK: Fuller took the risk of being called a rejected spinster when she reached out of her loneliness to Emerson. She too wanted a love relationship that offered more fulfillment than the traditional ways of her time. Emerson was so satisfied with the individualistic way of being of his time that he did not even understand what Fuller was reaching for.

ANNE: I'm sure that Joy too was a very lonely person when she took the tremendous risk of going to England to meet Lewis.

JACK: I believe that Jack was also a lonely person, but he didn't know it until Joy helped him learn what a real personal relationship could be. Without that relationship, he never would have experienced the depth of being that is present in *A Grief Observed* (Lewis 1976). I think he found out that he was lonely like the rest of us and that theological orthodoxy, no matter how reassuring, is no substitute for a relationship of love that you can enter with your whole being.

Mill and Taylor's Reaching for Dialogical Love and Finding Feminism

John Stuart Mill and Harriet Taylor hungered for a personal relationship that they could enter with their whole being. Taylor was lonely and unfulfilled because no one in her circles wanted to talk with a woman about the issues that deeply concerned her. Mill was not only lonely but felt unfulfilled because he was trying to live completely out of the intellectual side of his being. Mill and Taylor both were reaching out for more meaningful lives when they became friends in their early twenties. At that time, both of them were relatively unknown. Taylor was a house-wife and Mill's fame as a philosopher developed during their friendship and later marriage.

Mill was a prodigy who received an extensive education at an early age from his father. By the time he was twenty, he was well prepared for the fame he would eventually achieve as a philosopher and the leading interpreter of utilitarianism. But his education by his father had been devoted exclusively to his mind. Consequently, Mill, when only twenty years old, lamented that if he accomplished all that he planned to achieve, his life would still be empty because he would have nothing for which to live (Mill 1924, 94).

Fortunately, a Unitarian minister helped Mill find the meaning he lacked by suggesting to Taylor that she develop a friendship with Mill (Rose 1983, 103–104). Taylor had gone to the minister for counsel because of her disappointment with her marriage. She had been mar-ried for only four years, had two children she loved, and a husband who loved her and cared for her well. But she found him boring because of his lack of intellectual interest and abilities.

John and Harriet were well-suited to each other. Harriet found in John a stimulating intellectual companion, and John found in Harriet a companion who developed the neglected emotional and esthetic side of his life. John found Harriet very stimulating because her emotional and esthetic sensitivities had been integrated into her thought. In fact, John said of Harriet, "I had always wished for a friend whom I could admire wholly, without reservation and restriction, & I had now found one. To render this possible, it was necessary that the object of my admiration should be of a type very different from my own; should be a character preeminently of feeling, combined however as I had not in any other instance known it to be, with a vigorous & bold speculative intellect" (Mill 1961, 199).

The reason the two worked so well together is evident in Phyllis Rose's contrast between the two. "He spoke carefully. Give him facts, and he would sift them, weigh them, articulate possible interpretations, reach a conclusion. Where he was careful, she was daring. Where he was disinterested and balanced, she was intuitive, partial, and sure of herself. She concerned herself with goals and assumptions; he concerned himself with arguments. She was quick to judge and to generalize, and because he was not, he valued her intellectual style as bold and vigorous" (Rose, 106–107). She opened the world of poetry and art to him, and he so much appreciated her contributions to him that he thought of her as a better person than himself (107). Their relationship before their marriage was one of equality and sharing of being. It certainly was not a sexual relationship. They both had a low estimate of sexual activity and shared the "conviction that in each other they had found the highest companionship of which human beings were capable, a love compounded only of spirit and intellect, with no earthly dross, a love at the high end of the Platonic ladder—the greatest good life had to offer" (109).

During the over twenty years of their friendship, the couple received much criticism from those who did not understand their relationship. On one occasion when Mill arrived at a dinner party with Mrs. Taylor, it caused much consternation among their friends. When one of Mill's friends advised him to leave this compromising relationship, Mill refused to speak to him again. When Mill's father reproached his son for such a close relationship with another man's wife, Mill replied that his relationship and feeling toward Mrs. Taylor were not different than they would be for any competent man (116). However, their description of two weeks they spent alone together suggests a different kind of relationship. After the time together they confessed "we never could have been so near, so perfectly intimate, in any former circumstances—we never could have been together as we have been in numerable small relations and concerns." We could not "have spoken of all things, in all frames of mind with so much freedom and unreserve" (Hayek 1951, quoted in Rose, 112). It seems unlikely that "competent" men who were even close friends would have described their relationship in this way. Persons who were experiencing what we have called dialogical love could speak in this way of a relationship that intimate but not sexual. In commenting on their relationship, Mill, in his autobiography, assured his readers that he and Harriet's "relation to each other was one of strong affection and confidential intimacy only" (Mill 1961, 171).

Mill became enraged when his relationship with Harriet was interpreted as a sexual one. When Harriet's husband had died and Harriet and

John married, John's brother incurred his wrath for accusing him of being hypocritical for marrying when he had previously denied the need for marriage. John vehemently denounced his brother's criticism—because his brother insinuated that he and Harriet had been practitioners of the free love that his brother advocated. John was upset with his brother for believing that his relationship with Harriet rested on such a vulgar basis. The Mills "believed that their personal history proved something the world greatly needed proven; that rationality could be a more important bond between men and women than sensuality; that sex was less important in love than intellectual companionship; that sex could be done without altogether" (Rose, 122–123). They affirmed, "We distained, as every person not a slave of his animal appetites must do, the abject notion that the strongest & tenderest friendship cannot exist between a man & a woman without a sensual relation" (Mill 1961, 171).

Rose contends that there is no way of knowing whether their marriage involved a sexual relationship, but she is certain that "sex was not the binding element in Harriet's attachment to John and that John would not have approved its playing any part in his attachment to her" (Rose, 124). Regardless of how they developed their relationship after marriage, their twenty-year relationship prior to marriage clearly shows that an intellectual and spiritual relationship in which two people care for each other and contribute abundantly to each other's being could be developed without a sexual relationship.

JACK: Most feminists would applaud both their relationship and the advocacy of feminism that grew out of it. The Mills related to each other as equals. They did not believe in complementary relationships based on gender. Both recognized how their particular talents contributed to the other's life. Mill actually anticipated androgyny when he admired Taylor for having integrated the sensitivity and feelings usually associated with women with the intellectual ability and self-direction often associated with men.

ANNE: Feminists would not only applaud their relationship but their advocacy of the social and cultural reforms that make such a relationship possible. Their essay, *The Subjection of Women* (Mill

1980), is a classic work in feminist literature. I say their essay because, although it officially was authored by Mill, the themes developed are generally recognized as a joint undertaking.

JACK: I was taken by Mill's insight that women were doubly oppressed by the traditional expectation that they should be willing slaves. In contrast to a slave from whom the master only expects obedience, the traditional husband or other male not only expects obedience from his wife (or woman), but that she will obey him willingly. Thus, the husband doubly restricts the development of the wife by attempting to control not only his wife's behavior but her sentiments as well (Mill 1980, 14–15).

ANNE: I especially appreciated their treatment of how the woman becomes a willing slave. Men enculturate women to be willing slaves. Listen to this: "The masters of women wanted more than simple obedience, and they turned the whole force of education to effect their purpose. All women are brought up from the very earliest years in the belief that their ideal of character is the very opposite to that of men; not self-will and government by self-control, but submission and yielding to the control of others. All the moralities tell them that it is the duty of women, and all the current sentimentalities that it is their nature, to live for others, to make complete abnegation of themselves, and to have no life but in their affections" (15).

JACK: And if women do not want to become willing slaves, they soon learn why they had better be. According to the Mills, the livelihood of women and their position in society depends on their relationship to men (15). That was true of nineteenth-century England, but is it true of twentieth-century America in which you grew up?

ANNE: That depends on what part of the twentieth century you are talking about. My mother, myself, and my daughter have experienced economic independence, cultural freedom, and personal freedom differently. I might not be a good person to speak about women being forced into accepting the role of a willing slave.

JACK: I can't imagine you being a willing slave.

ANNE: But many of the women I have counseled have experienced great pressure to be willing slaves. Often that pressure took the form of physical, emotional, or sexual abuse.

JACK: Although our culture does not teach women or men that they ought to physically abuse each other, it has and often still does teach women to be other-serving and men to be self-seeking. That sets the stage for male dominance that can readily be perverted into overt abuse. It also makes it difficult for women to develop personal relationships with men inside or outside of marriage.

ANNE: Most marriage relationships when I was growing up were preceded by a courtship in which dominance and submissiveness were subtly built in.

JACK: Although we both felt those pressures, neither of us followed the pattern of dominance-submissiveness in developing our relationships with our spouses. We followed the traditional pattern only in that courtship, rather than friendship, preceded our marriages. Neither the Lewises nor the Mills followed that traditional approach. They not only rejected the dominance-submissiveness approach, but friendship, rather than traditional courtship, preceded their marriages.

ANNE: One of the couples we interviewed followed the same sequence that the Lewises and Mills did. We first became interested in interviewing them when one of them commented that he had married his best friend. They think that friendship rather than courtship should precede marriage.

David: In a relationship that starts out as romantic or physical or both so often there's other energies that I guess block a friendship or don't allow a friendship to develop, to blossom.

Shirley: If marriage begins with the romance and the sweetheart stuff and then there's the honeymoon phase that people talk about and all; once that's over then you have to either already have something or if you just started out with the passion and the attraction, then you have to work to develop it. . . . Either that or the relationship will probably end. . . . So it would seem, to me anyway . . . the best way to form a relationship would be as friends first, and I don't think a lot of people have that good fortune.

————

JACK: Those who start with friendship rather than romantic love are fortunate for another reason. Lovers in a romantic relationship exaggerate the good qualities of their lover, whereas friends tend to accept friends as they are.

ANNE: Certainly, the Lewises and the Mills began their relationships as friends. The Lewises eventually did include love in their relationship as well as friendship but that love was focused on the beloved and not on romance. In dialogical love, the focus is not only on the beloved, but the distinction between friend and lover actually vanishes.

JACK: One of our interviewees described that loss of the distinction between friend and lover. We have taken the liberty of attempting to set his description into a poetic interpretation that discloses how that distinction vanishes in relationships of dialogical love.

> Originally I loved Jane, my friend,
> Not Jane, my lover.
> Later I loved Jane as lovers love.
> But by then, the distinction between
> friend and lover no longer had meaning.
> There was no friend; there was no lover.
> Only Jane who I love. (George)

Chapter 6

I-THOU, PERSONAL, AND WE-RELATIONSHIPS

"I was having coffee in the faculty lounge with the wife of a good friend and colleague when the force of her personality and the intensity of our dialogue shook me. Then I realized that we had never encountered each other simply as persons. I had always regarded her as the wife of 'X.'" (Jack)

JACK: My quest for dialogical love began with the above insight. I'm still shocked when I recall relating to that person as the wife of "X." She eventually became my good friend but only after I began to relate to her as a person.

ANNE: I can understand why you would be shocked to discover that you related to her as the wife of "X." After having interpreted education in the light of Buber's I-Thou relationship, you discovered that you had ignored the implications of his thought for your relationships with women. Often the understanding we need is present in the thought of those we admire, but we don't recognize its full meaning in the world. It's always a shock when that new meaning leaps out of the book and informs our world.

JACK: I was shocked because I claimed to engage in the kind of dialogue advocated by Buber, in which you relate to your partners as you encounter them without putting them in a category and dealing with them categorically, such as the wife of "X." Martin

Buber (1970) would call such categorical relationships I-It in contrast to personal I-Thou relationships.

ANNE: And that means you had, in the past, consigned all women to the category of It! It's hard for me to think of you as such a male chauvinist.

JACK: I was but a very subtle one. At that time I was already a strong advocate of women's rights and equality. When someone asked Mary how she became a feminist, she responded, "By living with Jack."

ANNE: You lived your belief that women should be treated as equals in your relationship with Mary when the societal category of wife did not include equality. But you still were hemmed in by societal categories that limit personal relationships with women outside of marriage.

JACK: At that time, I challenged many societal categories that regulated human relationships, especially those that concerned race. No wonder I was shocked to discover that I related to women as the wife of "X."

ANNE: Actually, you didn't relate to women as the wife of "X." You related to women as your wife's husband, as all good husbands are supposed to do in our society. Husbands are not supposed to have close personal relationships with women—married or unmarried. And neither are wives permitted to have personal relationships with men. We women find this more limiting than men because we tend to value personal relationships more than men.

JACK: You sound like John Gray (1992). That's one of the reasons he claimed that women are from Venus and men are from Mars.

ANNE: Well, he may be right for men and women who have uncritically accepted traditional "male" and "female" ways of being. But I certainly think he is wrong in saying that men and women can learn to better communicate and relate to each other by recognizing and responding to each other categorically.

JACK: Gray seems to believe that before I can communicate well with members of the other sex, I must put them in the category of man or woman and respond to them categorically rather than personally.

ANNE: Having known your mother and heard all the storie.
father, I can see why you would reject responding cate
to men and women, at least to the categories that Gray use.

JACK: My father was the sensitive one in our family. He responde.
personally to all people and had a knack for recognizing good
qualities in people, especially those that were unrecognized by
others. My mother used to get mad at him for not standing up
for his rights in conflicts with other people rather than smooth-
ing out troubled relationships. Mom was the person of principle and the disciplinarian in our family. In disciplining, her move
of last resort was to use her hairbrush. One of the jokes of our
family is that we didn't know until we were grown that a hairbrush was supposed to be applied to the top of your body.

ANNE: But I remember that in the seniors' apartment house where your
mother lived, she was affectionately known as "The Lady." Certainly, in our church, she was thought of as a well-dressed, ele-
gant lady.

JACK: And Dad was a man's man. He managed a crew of wild travel-
ing salesmen, played cards with them, smoked cigars, partied with
them, and beat them in athletic contests. His crew outsold all
other crews in the company and was a recruiting ground for company sales managers. Each of my parents, like most people I
know, combined so-called male and female virtues and ways of
being. I can't imagine them relating to each other on the basis
of gender by learning how the other sex thinks and operates so
that they could communicate and work with each other. I always
thought my parents did that pretty well by ignoring gender prescriptions and just being themselves.

ANNE: I'll bet the success that Gray claims in getting couples to communicate has been limited to those who were rigidly socialized
into male and female roles. But I think he is leading them in
the wrong direction. We need less categorical relationships and
more personal ones.

JACK: Certainly Buber (1970) would agree with that. Somewhere in
his writings he says that the direction that has been given to us
by past generations is losing its force, and we are now called

upon to take personal responsibility for directing our lives and relationships.

ANNE: Taking responsibility for our lives and forming relationships personally rather than categorically does not mean that in our personal response to each other, we won't encounter the past effects of having been enculturated as male or female. Relating to someone personally means that you encounter that person as he or she is present to you, rather than placing him or her in a category, such as man or woman, and responding categorically. When I respond to you personally, I often encounter a person with a strong sense of justice who is willing to fight for the rights of others. In our society, that's considered a male trait.

JACK: But you've forgotten that that fierce sense of justice and rights came from my mother! Dad also believed that all people ought to be treated equally and well, but in his case, that came out of his warm affection for other people, as did his tolerance of difference in others. I believe that's considered a feminine approach to justice and equality. Gray (1992) tends to dismiss differences like those of my parents by calling them role reversals. I'm not sure what that accounts for other than saying that they don't fit into societal categories for men and women as he interprets them. I wonder what Gray would make of relationships like ours in which there is no ordering by gender roles.

The Personal and Categorical: Buber

Buber is famous for contrasting I-It and I-Thou relations. In I-It relationships, persons respond to each other categorically, as Jack did before he recognized the implications of Buber's dialogue for relationships between men and women who are married but not to each other. In an I-Thou relationship you respond to the other as that person is present to you. For example, when your friend is upset, you respond immediately by listening to what has upset your friend, and you comfort him or her. In an I-It relationship, you respond to the person categorically. For example, if you're male and your female friend is upset, you might think, "It's alright for me to go to her house alone and hug her sympathetically as long as I pat her on the back while I am doing it." I-Thou relationships are relationships of immediate and unmediated response. I-It relationships are relationships of detachment and categorically determined response. In I-Thou relationships the other person is known directly through personal encounter and response. I-Thou relationships are mutual relationships in which persons freely respond to each other as they are present to each other. I-It relationships are one-sided relationships in which one person or society determines the relationship. I-Thou relationships can never be completely defined because they are freely and continually developed in an ongoing relationship. I-It relationships require clear definition that determine the nature of the relationship. In I-Thou relationships, each partner has his or her own worth whereas in an I-It relationship the worth of one person is determined by the usefulness of that person to another person or society. You enter the I-Thou relationship with your whole being, whereas you enter an I-It relationship with only that part of your being that is appropriate. "Just" friends and affair relationships are examples of this partial being. "Just" friend relationships categorically reject sexual relationships, whereas affairs exist solely for the purpose of sexual-romantic relations.

Buber contends that we usually form relationships categorically rather than personally. In contrast to comfortable prescribed categorical relationships, personal relationships require reaching out to a person as present and responding to that presence freely and courageously. The meaning of presence is difficult to articulate positively, but it is easy to grasp negatively. For example, a daughter waits for her father to become engrossed in a basketball game in which his favorite team is playing for the conference championship, and then at a crucial point in the game, she says very softly, "Daddy, can I stay out until two A.M. tonight?" The father says, "Yes, yes, of course!" Then later when he reprimands her for staying out so late, she says, "You said I could stay out until two A.M.!" And he replies, "Yes, but you asked me at a time and in a way that assured I wouldn't be present." The positive side of presence is much harder to illustrate, but all those engaged in personal relationships have experienced being fully present to each other or being "really there" with each other. The inadequacy of language for describing this experience is probably the reason that one interpreter of Buber called I-Thou relationships ineffable, in contrast to a categorical relationship in which clear definitions are possible (Friedman 1956, 95).

Categorical relationships are defined by society. The cultural designations for relationships between men and women who are married but not to each other generally have been categorized as "just" friends or as affairs. Both relationships receive their designation by reference to sexual relationship and not to personal involvement with each other. No one would say of two close friends of the same sex, who are not homosexual, that they were "just" friends because they did not engage in sexual relationships. They would simply be spoken of as close friends or good friends because of the quality of their relationship. In categorical thinking, persons are placed in a societal category and the relationship is determined by that category. Categorical thinking can lead to strange claims when a relationship that is personal is placed in categorical logic. For example, a husband says to his wife, "Of course I love you, you are my wife." Most wives want to feel that their husbands love them as the person they are, not as a logical consequence of their being in the category of wife. Categorical thinking, however, can make sense when you are dealing with public obligations. A judge says to a father who is delinquent in his child support, "You are this child's father, therefore you will contribute to her support."

Buber recognized that I-It categorical relationships are necessary for societal living. He contended that it was impossible to live in an I-Thou relationship all of the time or even most of the time. He felt that those who continually lived in I-Thou relationships would burn out. He did believe, however, that you could live in I-It relationships all of the time, but if you did, you were not really human. "In all the seriousness of truth, listen; without It a human being cannot live. But whoever lives only with that is not human" (Buber, 85). If Buber is right, people live in an everyday I-It relationship most of the time, but the I-Thou, the intense personal relationship, breaks through and transforms the relationship and the person. It is this transformation that makes us fully human beings. To put this in our language, when the I-Thou relationship breaks through the conventional I-It relationships that control how the sexes relate to each other, the partners experience abundant being that transforms their way of being.

Treating love relationships categorically makes love appear static. Actually, the experience of love is transient; it comes and goes. When partners who really attune to each other respond to each other's presence by saying, "I love you" over and over, they do so in recognition of love's coming into being now. They become ecstatically present to each other. This way of being present is always mutual and always involves the whole being of each partner. The worth of each partner is confirmed by the way the other responds. Since this relationship is always free-flowing and interactive, it is impossible to describe it adequately in the objective language used to describe static things.

Persons cannot know each other personally as static things. The way they are present to each other constantly changes in an I-Thou encounter, as does their response to that encounter. That's why you cannot convey understanding of a person, especially someone you love, through static concepts or categories. The only way to convey understanding of that person is through stories that disclose his or her way of being in personal interaction with you. A striking example of conveying this kind of knowledge was in the film, *Same Time Next Year* (1978). The leading characters in this film met in the same week for many years and developed a relationship similar to dialogical love. They came to know each other's spouse through telling stories that revealed their spouse's way of being with them. We have attempted to help our readers recognize dialogical love relationships by our own stories, imaginative stories, stories told us by others, and stories from literature. These stories, unlike categories that define by lists of characteristics, describe particular interactions between persons that reveal the way one person responds to another person in a given situation. The story does not attempt to say what this person is but rather how this person relates to another person.

ANNE: Buber is not only known for articulating the difference between I-Thou and I-It but for articulating dialogue as well. How does dialogue relate to I-Thou and I-It relationships?

JACK: Dialogue is the way of relating in an I-Thou relationship and monologue is the way of relating in an I-It relationship. That difference was evident in Emerson's delivering a lecture in a group formed for dialogical exchange. It's no wonder that Emerson could not understand Fuller's invitation to a dialogical love relationship.

ANNE: Emerson seems uncomfortable with open, fluid relationships involving free response to personal presence. As I remember his essay on friendship, it's more concerned with doings that illustrate characteristics than with relationships. Does Buber distinguish between I-It and I-Thou by giving characteristics?

JACK: Buber describes ways of being with another person and with the world. But for that way of being to have substance, you need stories that convey particular relationships. For example, while we have not defined dialogue categorically, we have given examples of dialogical love throughout the book. An example of the difference in categorical definition and conveying meaning through stories of relationship is the story of the Good Samaritan. A scribe asked Jesus to give him a definition of neighbor in terms of characteristics that he could use to direct his behavior. Instead, Jesus conveys the meaning of neighbor through the Samaritan's care of an injured man.

ANNE: When I think of dialogue, I usually think of relating to each other in interactive speech. But your example of the Good Samaritan's nursing care for the injured man is an example of dialogue through touch.

JACK: If dialogue is the way of I-Thou relationships, it includes much more than speech. It involves responding to each other with the whole lived body.

ANNE: Then dialogue would include touching, hugging, laughing, crying, jostling—the whole range of bodily expression.

JACK: Dialogical relationships bring into being attraction to, affection for, care of, and those ineffable qualities that we associate with love. This relationship of dialogical love is experienced as a oneness that is more a belonging together than a union. Dialogical love relationships bring deep meaning to your being, ecstatic joy that makes life special, and assurance that what you are becoming is good.

The Social and the Personal: Macmurray

Buber's distinction between I-It categorical relations and I-Thou personal relationships sets a context for John Macmurray's criticism of traditional categorical relationships between men and women. For Macmurray, the societal categories of gender roles, marriage, and romantic love inhibit personal relationships between men and women, foster emotional dishonesty, and deny the equality of men and women.

Macmurray (1935) argues against restricting personal relationships between men and women to either "just" friend relationships or courtship and marriage relationships. In a "just" friend relationship, men and women "behave to one another as if the difference of sex was non-existent," and in the courtship/marriage relationship, "they are so aware of the difference that other considerations are crowded out" (113–114). He contends that "there is only one proper ground of relationship between any two human beings, and that is mutual friendship. Difference of sex may make the friendship easier or more difficult of achievement, but it cannot make any difference in principle" (134). Mutual friendship is the proper ground because "men and women must meet and enter into relationships on the personal level—not as male and female, but as human beings" (134). Macmurray opposes any restrictions that infringe on the freedom of men and women to develop their own personal relationships. Prophetically, he asserted in the early 1930s that the relationship between men and women was "perhaps the most important of all the problems which this generation is called upon to face," and he further claimed that it was a new problem "in the history of civilization" (118). Today most of us would not call it a new problem, but we certainly would call it one of the most difficult problems we still face. Since Macmurray wrote, the increase in sexual freedom and the rise of the feminist movement have made this problem a more urgent one. Macmurray, however, was ahead of his time in that he anticipated both developments in a way that makes his philosophy relevant to our situation. In fact, when we first became friends, we found Macmurray's philosophy most helpful.

Macmurray's treatment of the relationship between the sexes is based on his distinction between social and personal life. Social life, according to

Macmurray, is essentially a functional structure through which people are arranged in a hierarchy according to their contribution to the purpose of the group. In contrast, personal life has no end beyond itself. Participants share in personal life as equals. Individual differences enrich relationships rather than rank them. Personal relationships free persons to be themselves. In contrast, social relationships limit freedom in order to achieve the purpose of the group. In addition, social relationships can only be entered into with that part of the self that fosters the purpose of the group; whereas, personal relationships are entered into with the whole self (94–106).

Macmurray contends that all social relations should be judged by their contributions to personal life. The purpose of social life is to provide a societal context in which personal life will flourish. "No political or economic form, no social institution however hoary with ancient associations, has any value in itself. It is a means to an end. The organization of life can only be justified if it makes possible the equality and freedom of human beings in the personal life" (111). The personal life, which social institutions are to promote, is a relationship of equality and freedom "in which we are seeking to accept one another and to be accepted for what we are, so that we may be ourselves and express ourselves for one another" (105–106).

There are two primary societal infringements on developing personal relationships between men and women, according to Macmurray. The first is assigning complementary roles to men and women in which men specialize in individuality and intellect and women in unity and emotion. He contends that such specialization cripples the emotional life of men and stunts the intellectual life of women (118–121). He anticipated the contemporary idea of codependency, arguing that such dependency, especially when dictated by society, destroys freedom and causes persons to lose their integrity (135). The second way Macmurray contends that society controls personal relationships between men and women is controlling sexual desire through the institution of marriage and the romanticizing of love. He maintains that determining the legitimacy of sexual relationships by limiting them to marriage fosters immoral relationships between the sexes. In traditional marriage, relationships are sanctioned by societal regulation and not by right personal relationships

(121–125). Romantic love attempts to control sexual appetites by fostering emotional dishonesty. Romantic love inclines us to attribute qualities to others that they do not possess so that they may be worthy of our love. Romantic love sets women on pedestals in ways that "assert their inferiority and so insult their humanity" (138–139).

Macmurray is not advocating views of sexual relations that are common in our time. He is not saying, "Do your own thing as long as you don't hurt someone else" or "Enough of this romantic nonsense; sex is merely an appetite." Instead, he contends that sex is raised above the level of appetite when a personal relationship transforms sexual relationship into communion. The focus of communion is enjoyment of each other, whereas sexual appetite uses the other for its own gratification. Macmurray contends that "in all enjoyment there is a choice between enjoying the other and enjoying yourself through the instrumentality of the other. The first is the enjoyment of love, the second is the enjoyment of lust" (141). Macmurray contends that sexual relationship is only one possible expression of love, and it is not fundamentally different from other expressions of love (139). All forms of love share in common that they have no end beyond themselves because the essential nature of human beings is "to share their experience, to understand one another, to find joy and satisfaction in living together; in expressing and revealing themselves to one another" (98). It follows from this interpretation of love that sexual relationships are not the defining or even a necessary part of a love relationship. Sexual relationships are an option that may be included in a personal relationship, but this choice must be one based on emotional honesty, freedom, and equality. He contends that love is the basis of personal relationships but that love "may or may not include sexual attraction" (136).

ANNE: When we met, you had already written a paper on Macmurray. You were so enthused about his treatment of the relationship between men and women that I was surprised how much of your paper was critical of aspects of his thought.

JACK: Don't remind me of that paper! I can't believe that I was so critical of Macmurray. After all, his treatment of the relationship between men and women opened a new possibility for me.

Rather than developing that new way, I fell back into the old habits that were drilled into us in graduate school of criticizing the scholar's thought rather than exploring the possibilities opened by his thought.

ANNE: What new possibilities should you have developed?

JACK: The possibility of developing personal relationships between men and women rather than romantic or sexual relationships.

ANNE: When we first met, you certainly were turned on to developing personal relationships and that made it possible for us to develop the relationship we have with each other.

JACK: Those who have read this far in our book should realize that Macmurray's interpretation of personal life between the sexes has informed our relationship. There is a sense in which we are doing now what I should have done in that original paper. Macmurray makes personal life and its development fundamental for human beings and evaluates social institutions by their contribution to personal life. That's quite different from the way you and I were taught to think of the relationship between the sexes when we were growing up. We believed that we should form romantic love relationships with the opposite sex first as courtship and eventually as marriage relationships that would eventuate in family life. We were not enculturated to cultivate personal relationships between the sexes, but some of us did in our courtship and marital relationships. I'm amazed at how well Mary and I developed a personal relationship given our cultural expectations and the contingencies of getting through graduate school, raising a family, building a home, and all the rest. During those years I don't remember thinking that romantic relationships and marital relationships restricted the development of personal relationships.

ANNE: But you would have if you wanted to develop a personal relationship with a member of the opposite sex outside of marriage. The societal arrangements for the sexes that we grew up with were aimed at restricting personal relationships between the sexes outside of marriage relationships, as you and I now know. You and I found Macmurray's thought exciting because it opened possibilities for personal relationships outside of marriage. He issued a call for men and women to pursue authentic being in their relationships rather than allowing those relationships to be determined by societal restrictions.

JACK: Pursuing authentic being is not just blocked by restrictions. Many people value the comfort of everyday traditional ways of being so much that they are not open to new ways of being.

ANNE: Remember the story our friend, Ken West, told the readers of his column in the local paper to illustrate why some people fail to, "Seize the moment when a door opens" (West 1997)?

We took the torn screen out of the door. Only the frame of the door remained. To run to freedom Old Yeller, our cat, needed only to leap through the opening. But he sat there and gazed through the open door frame, just as he did when the screen prevented his liberation. An outside cat, Old Yeller was imprisoned inside by his own imagination. . . .

Old Yeller's mind kept him inside. He saw his world as it had always been. He was not ready to see the open door. . . . The door is open. Hearing the call, many charge through the open door and see the world and live in it differently forever.

Others, like Old Yeller, continue to see the world as they always have. They may envy those who dance in freedom, but they cannot give up the world as they have always known it and lived in it. (West 1997, B1)

JACK: The screen of marriage can block personal relationships between men and women. But as we both know, marriage relationships can foster personal relationships. Simon and Meilaender both show why marriage can be the ideal relationship for fostering authentic personal love. Romantic love also can function as a screen, but Solomon contends romantic love relationships are ideal contexts for developing self-esteem. Personally, I think he overdoes it, but I'm glad that I was involved in some very positive romantic relationships when I was young. The fact that romantic relationships and marriage can be used to foster emotional dishonesty and restrict freedom does not mean that they cannot foster personal relationships.

ANNE: There you go criticizing Macmurray again, but I agree with that criticism. Macmurray goes too far, but marriage and romantic love can be as restrictive as he says. In fact, I counsel with women whose experience shows that marriage and romantic love not only can inhibit love but can crush it. Macmurray is certainly right in contending that we women have been victimized by being socialized to express emotion and promote harmony rather than being assertive and thoughtful.

JACK: I couldn't agree more. But I believe that complementary relationships freely chosen can foster, rather than inhibit, abundant being. Such relationships allow the partners to make the most of their inclinations and talents. For example, you have just filled the screen of the computer with great ease, whereas I plod along and fill the screen with mistakes. Some people are more talented than others and enjoy using their talents. I find complementary relationships freeing rather than limiting when the partners contribute what they do best rather than wasting time bungling tasks they don't enjoy. I originally criticized Macmurray for not recognizing that freely chosen complementary relationships are freeing. In so doing, I failed to do justice to his main contribution, namely, complementary relationships should not be assigned on the basis of sex.

ANNE: Yes! As you said, I'm typing not because I am a women but because you have spastic fingers and I have agile ones. You have an agile mind but you'd better not say I have a spastic one!

JACK: I will be satisfied if you say my mind is more agile than yours. I will consider that a high compliment. But seriously, I do value Macmurray's rejection of complementary relationships based on sex. I would prefer saying gender rather than sex, but that distinction was not generally in use when Macmurray wrote.

ANNE: Regardless of whether gender or sex is more appropriate, we do relate to each other simply as persons, with no reference to gender or sex.

JACK: Macmurray certainly would applaud a man and a woman who relate to each other simply as persons and reject all gender prescriptions that limit their free expression and personal development.

ANNE: I'm sure he would approve our free and equal relationship through which we, as he advocates, share our experience, understand one another, find joy and satisfaction in being together; and express and reveal ourselves to one another (98).

We-Relationships: Schutz

JACK: The personal face-to-face relationships that Macmurray advocates foster what Schutz calls we-relationships. Our we-relationship causes eyebrows to raise when the *we* expresses a personal, rather than professional, relationship.

ANNE: Our friends and colleagues have no difficulty responding to the *we* of our professional work. I'm often asked, "How is the book you and Jack are writing coming along?" Then I tell them how much we have or have not accomplished.

JACK: When I respond, I usually tell them more than they want to know. I talk about what and how we are thinking about a certain issue. That often terminates the discussion.

ANNE: That use of *we* is intriguing. What does it mean when either of us says, "We think?" The meaning of *I think* is clear. If I said "You think," I'm sure you'd respond, "Why don't you ask me what I think?" But I don't think you would respond to *we think* by saying, "Why don't you ask me what we think?"

JACK: When we think together in dialogue as we are now doing, we come to know both what and how each other thinks. When one of us says "We think," that partner is confident that the other shares in that belief or in that way of thinking. Also, the we-think assertion assumes that the other person will challenge the we-thinking if it does not express the way or content of his or her thinking.

ANNE: We-think language and talk can be stifling. I can think of marriage relationships in which one partner always speaks for the

other in a way that inhibits the free expression of the other partner and sometimes verbally abuses him or her. The *we think* of
dialogical love is communicated to others by partners who
encourage and enable each other to speak for themselves as well
as for we. Relating to each other in that context is the primary
reason that neither of us hesitates to say, "We think."

JACK: We-relationships deserve to be thought through more deeply
than we have up to now. No one that I know of generates more
thought concerning we-relationships than Alfred Schutz (1967)
and his interpreter Richard Zaner (1981).

Schutz defines we-relationships as a "face-to-face relationship in
which the partners are aware of each other and sympathetically participate in each other's lives" (Schutz 1969, 164). In we-relationships the
partners relate to each other concretely by bringing into the relationship
their own personal characteristics and ways of being with each other
and the world. These ways of being are affected by sedimented meanings inherited from the past and shared with others in our culture. For
Schutz, these typified meanings are most forcefully and clearly evident
in language (Natanson 1986, 45–47). Schutz's insight accounts for why
such accepted categories as lovers and "just" friends can inform and limit
we-relationships between men and women.

When we-relationships do not fit into culturally defined ways of
being, the partners often seek meaning from each other by contrasting
what they experience with defined cultural ways of being. Schutz points
out that knowing another person requires societal knowledge of persons
in general and personal knowledge of this particular person. We bring a
whole stock of previously constituted knowledge into our relationship
with one another. This knowledge includes both knowledge of what
another person is as such and any specific knowledge of the person in
question. "It includes knowledge of other people's interpretive schemes,
their habits, and their language. It includes knowledge of the taken-for-
granted in-order-to and because-motives of others as such and of this
person in particular" (Schutz, 169). To relate to each other, we need to
know the cultural ways of others in general and the particular ways of
this person.

When I attune to your experience, I become conscious of your lived experience, not just my own. This attuning to your experience makes we-experience possible. "And when I am face to face with someone, my knowledge of him is increasing from moment to moment. My ideas of him undergo continuous revision as the concrete experience unfolds. . . . As I watch his face and his gestures and listen to the tone of his voice, I become aware of much more than what he is deliberately trying to communicate to me" (169).

From living through experience together, according to Schutz, we can constitute our world. "The world of the We is not private to either of us, but is our world, the one common intersubjective world which is right there in front of us. It is only from the face-to-face relationship, from the common lived experience of the world in the We, that the intersubjective world can be constituted" (171). We constitute and expand our world by questioning each other as we live together. These questions concern both the interpretive schemes used to make sense of our common world and the schemes used to make sense of our own personal lives. By inquiring into your interpretive schemes, "I can correct, expand, and enrich my own understanding of you. This becoming-aware of the correctness or incorrectness of my understanding of you is a higher level of the We-experience" (171).

One of the most important interpretive schemes for knowing another person, for Schutz, is "a set of genuine because- or in-order-to motives" (171). When we interact with persons we do not know well, we expect motives that are the ones generally assumed in our society. In contrast, when we interact with those with whom we have "a higher level of the we-experience," the motives we expect of our partner grow out of our mutual awareness of each other's motives as we have come to know each other from dialoguing and acting together.

In we-relationships we not only share a world together and come to know each other intimately, but according to Zaner, we attune to each other to reach a unity and a harmony in which "in Schutz's delightful phrase, 'we make music together'" (Zaner, 1981, 236). That harmony, according to Zaner, will "evoke that wonder *over and at* 'our' common endeavor of working together" and we will experience "a kind of 'depth' and . . . 'warmth'" (236). The warmth and depth of we-relationships leads us beyond our present relationship with "promises of the 'still to come'" (237) and helps us become more fully ourselves. "The time and space of love, of friendship, of caring, is a time and space at once 'far' yet 'close': The 'near' and the 'warm' which are yet something which 'go beyond' us, are 'deeper' than us. . . . Thus do we prize our love, our friendship, 'beyond' even ourselves. For thanks to it . . . 'I' am fully myself, within the relationship itself wherein 'you' are fully yourself" (237).

ANNE: I like that—a we-relationship of warmth and depth in which we become more fully ourselves. Before I met you, I appreciated warmth of being and believed that all people ought to strive to become fully themselves. I have gained much philosophical depth from working with you. But please note that in Dick's (Zaner) treatment of depth, the depth of being is not primarily that of knowing. If I read our we-relationship rightly, we both have become much deeper in Dick's existential sense of being. That's what we mean when we talk about the abundance of being that has come through our we-relationship.

JACK: We both have been blessed with abundant being, but in truth, I think in that sense, you have become deeper.

ANNE: Do you mean I have become deeper than you? If so, I doubt it, but thanks. Or that I have become deeper than I was? If so, that's true.

JACK: I think you have become deeper than I and much deeper than you were. The existential depth we are talking about has to do with intimacy and affection and the felt sense of how we relate to each other in our world. We constitute our world and thoroughly enjoy living with each other in that world. When we speak and live out of our we-world, our we-language that discloses our world also reveals our feelings toward each other. Schutz makes evident why many people would become upset with our culturally *illegitimate* we-relationship.

ANNE: Those of our readers who do not understand our use of living together may misunderstand our meaning. Some people who reside together do not actually live together. We live together even though we don't reside together. By living together, we mean that we come into being existentially through our we-relationship.

JACK: Such closeness between a man and a woman in our society is only expected from husband and wife. In these relationships, the "in-order-to" has a specific meaning. Traditionally, couples were married "in-order-to" have legitimate intimate sexual relationships which hopefully would produce children who would be raised over a long life together and eventually provide grandchildren. We both are fortunate in that we have lived in we-relationships with our spouses for well over forty years, have raised families, and are grandparents, and I'm a great grandfather.

ANNE: You and I have constituted our own we-world from which we speak to others concerning what we value, strive for, appreciate, and hope for. The amount and quality of time that must be shared in order to constitute a we-world is beyond societal expectations for men and women who are not married to each other. In our society, we cannot legitimately relate to each other primarily in-order-to enjoy each other in a relationship with the quantity and quality of time required to constitute a we-world from which to live.

JACK: Even in professional societies where our we-relationship is generally accepted, the personal quality of our relationship raises questions. The leader of one scholarly society, who knows both you and Mary, speaks to me of "my two women."

ANNE: How do you feel about that?

JACK: Well, I don't like it. I would never speak of either of you possessively as *my woman*. I don't relate to *two women*, but to you and to Mary. Further, *my two women* implies that my relationships with you and Mary are the same, just because you are women.

ANNE: The time we spend together is justified by others as time spent on thinking and writing, even when we are not working professionally but simply enjoying each other's presence. We do, of course, enjoy each other's presence when we are thinking and writing together, and our scholarship was spawned by that enjoyment and the desire to share its fruits. I guess that means that the legitimacy of our being together is academically questionable.

Seriously, working together enhances our relationship and gives us that special enjoyment that comes when the we of a professional relationship is the we of a personal one.

JACK: What disturbs me is that persons who could experience abundant being together have great difficulty doing so because the legitimacy of their relationship is not recognized in our society. Unlike us, they often do not have a legitimate way of being together through which they can cultivate their relationship in the way that we have.

ANNE: I don't see why close friends, who are men and women and are married, but not to each other, need any reason for being together other than they enjoy each other's company, especially when they love each other personally.

JACK: Schutz, by pointing out how sedimentary cultural ways affect our relationships, makes evident why such relationships need to gain societal legitimacy. Without such legitimacy, only hardy souls will engage in individual acts that, as Buber says somewhere, "ventilate the system." We and others treated in this book have or are engaging in such acts. We hope these acts will eventually foster cultural change that will legitimize personal we-relationships between men and women outside of courtship and marriage.

Chapter 7

WHY DIALOGICAL LOVE?

ANNE: Buber, Macmurray, and Schutz give us three interrelated ways of interpreting dialogical love. We can articulate dialogical love as an I-Thou relationship rather than a categorical one. Certainly, it is a personal relationship rather than a social one, and persons in dialogical love relationships are in we-relationships.

JACK: Schutz's we-relationship does more than affirm the we-ness experienced in relationships of dialogical love. He shows how the general sedimented ways of being of society and the particular ways of being of partners are involved in we-relationships.

ANNE: But if we only act out of sedimented ways of being, particular or societal, are we not relating to each other as I-It? Buber's I-Thou relationship means that we respond to each other as we are immediately present to each other.

JACK: Acting *only* out of sedimented ways of being would squelch dialogical love relationships. But when we immediately relate to each other's presence, the general sedimented ways of our culture are present as are our particular sedimented ways of being. When you love someone, you love those particular sedimented ways of being—at least most of them. But a person is more than sedimented ways of being. The personal, as Buber interprets it, has to do with encountering that more as it enlivens, challenges, and redirects sedimented ways of being.

ANNE: What I value in our relationship is how often we are present to each other as I and Thou and how rarely we coast along in

111

sedimented ways of being—societal or individual. But Schutz is right in contending that sedimented ways of being are always present in personal encounters, but they are not *the* presence.

JACK: By suggesting that we look for the *in-order-to* of sedimented ways of being, Schutz helps us understand why people in our society are inclined to put couples who are married but not to each other into "just" friend or affair categories. The in-order-to of affairs is to have sexual relationships. The in-order-to of "just" friends is less clear. It would make no sense to say that couples became friends in-order-to not have sex. The in-order-to of "just" friends may be society's way of heading off love relationships. Remember how Lewis and Simon and some of those interviewed by Werking feared that close friendships between men and women would become lover relationships? "Just" friend labeling may be another way that society controls personal relationships between the sexes in addition to those treated by Macmurray.

ANNE: Macmurray contends that societal prescriptions designed to restrict sexual relationships curtail personal relationships. That runs counter to the purpose of society that, according to Macmurray, is to foster personal relationships. Personal relationships are relationships of freedom and equality in which *persons* choose how they relate to each other. The essence of personal relationships is responding to others freely, uninhibited by societal prescriptions. Macmurray's interpretation of personal relations sounds very much like Buber's.

JACK: They are very similar, but Macmurray is focusing on personal relationships between men and women, whereas Buber is describing all personal relationships. Dialogical love is well described by Macmurray's articulation of personal relationships between men and women, when personal means I-Thou relationships in which partners respond to each other as they are immediately present to each other. Schutz helps us to see that even when we are immediately present to each other, our presence includes societal and individual sedimented ways of being and that understanding these ways can facilitate personal encounters. He also shows that personal relationships develop as we-relationships through which couples constitute a shared lived world.

ANNE: Now we have three philosophical interpretations of personal love that support our articulation of dialogical love. Dialogue is the way of relating as I and Thou, of forming personal relationships that are free and equal, and of cultivating we-relationships free of the tendency to control. Now we need to consider how dialogical love relates to friendship and love and specifically to intergendered love. How can dialogical love be distinguished from love and friendship when interpreted personally as Lewis and May do?

JACK: Lewis and May both contend that friendship and lover relationships are personal ways of being together. Being together is the essence of dialogical love when being is meant existentially. The way we sometimes express it is that "we be's together." I'm sure glad that Erazim Kohak, our philosopher friend who was raised in Czechoslovakia, pointed out that he thought southern black Americans say it right in the way they employ be's.

ANNE: Lewis and May seem to treat the problem of how to distinguish love and friendship from each other as a problem inherent in relationships of personal love. Lewis structured friendship as a side-by-side relationship in which friends have common orientations and pursuits. He contrasts friendship with love relationships in which persons meet in a face-to-face relationship. Although it's clear how love relationships are personal, it's less clear how side-by-side relationships can be personal.

JACK: Lewis's insistence that friendship is always a side-by-side relationship gets in the way of interpreting friendship as a love, as does his tendency to treat friendship as a man-to-man relationship and Eros as a man-to-woman relationship. I shutter to think how persons with a homosexual orientation respond to his treatment of Eros. I hope we have not been that insensitive in considering Eros from our heterosexual perspective.

ANNE: May's personal face-to-face interpretation of friendship is a more adequate interpretation of friendship as personal love than Lewis's side-by-side one. But if we adopt May's face-to-face interpretation of friendship, we still face the problem of how to distinguish friendship from Eros.

JACK: Even if May's contention is true that friendship does not include ecstasy in the way that love does, that claim fails to make a satisfactory distinction between them. But ecstatic exaltation can be present in all forms of personal love. In personal love, ecstasy comes from being fully in the presence of the other person rather than from being in love. Personal love is different from *being in love* in that being in love can take you away from the particularity of your lover.

ANNE: Shirley certainly believed that romantic love takes you away from personal encounter. Remember how she observed that after romantic love fades, those who haven't formed friendships will often terminate their marriage. That sounds like Solomon's contention that a romantic love relationship cannot last without friendship. When Shirley and David talked about friendship as the best basis of marriage, I believe that what they call friendship is really dialogical love. But if it isn't, it at least shows how difficult it is to distinguish friendship and love in personal love relationships.

JACK: Simon tries to make that distinction by contrasting personal destinies with *we* destinies. The primary thrust of friendship is fostering each other's personal destiny, but close personal friends, secondarily, develop a *we* destiny. In contrast, the primary thrust of a lover relationship is to seek union in a common *we* destiny, but lovers, secondarily, foster each other's personal destiny.

ANNE: It seems to me that whether couples focus on *we* destiny or on personal destinies should vary with the persons involved and their situation, rather than being determined by societal category and sanction. Dialogical love frees partners to decide whether to stress we destiny or personal destiny or to place less emphasis on destiny and more on cultivating personal relationships.

JACK: Simon's stress on gender, rather than personal relationships, is the reason she uses the term *intergender friendship*. That term could have been used by Lewis in *The Four Loves* because of his contention, like Simon's, that love disrupts friendship between the sexes. Even May, with his personal interpretation of both friendship and love, seems to interpret personal love as a gendered relationship.

ANNE: Both Eros and friendship become personal love relationships when partners respond to each other dialogically rather than on a gender basis. Lewis had moved decidedly in that direction when he reinterpreted his relationship with Joy after her death. The distinctions between friendship and love and male and female became meaningless as his personal love relationship with Joy flourished.

JACK: In dialogical love relationships, friendship and Eros lose their meaning as existential distinctions that determine the way men and women "be's" together.

ANNE: They lose their meaning as existential distinctions, but do they lose their societal meaning? Don't they incline people to force personal love relationships into societal categories, thereby distorting them?

JACK: Yes, and Solomon helps us understand why. Remember how he questions "why we are so adamant about distinguishing friendship from romantic love, that is, apart from the initial obvious fact that the latter is intrinsically sexual and the former is not." Then he asks, "Why should this be the case? Perhaps we place an excessive emphasis on sexual relations? Or maybe we have an emasculated notion of friendship" (Solomon 1981, 10).

ANNE: Emasculated! Why doesn't he just say, as the dictionary defines emasculate, "deprived of virility, strength or vigor" (*American Heritage Dictionary*)?

JACK: I'm glad he said emasculated! That's exactly what I think of "just friend" relationships. In order to rid the relationship of any hint of sex, it is called "just" friend and in the process, friendship is robbed of its virility, strength, and vigor. It also shows inadvertently how "hung up" we are on gendered ordering and sex. The reason we go to such lengths to distinguish love relationships from friendship is that it is one way of controlling relationships between the sexes.

ANNE: When we think of relationships as dialogical love, that obsession becomes absurd and that control unwarranted.

JACK: Dialogical love relationships cannot be neatly divided into Eros and friendship. Those who make such distinctions often are trying to preserve traditional gendered ways of thinking about the relationship between men and women. The recognized relationship between men and women traditionally has been courtship-to-marriage, focused on sexual relationship and gendered prescription of how the sexes should relate to each other. Men and women can relate to each other legitimately outside of this context only in a "just" friend relationship—that not only means the absence of sex but, as Solomon says, an emasculated version of friendship.

ANNE: Emasculated certainly expresses the loss of vigor, virility, and strength in "just" friend relationships, but I'm not going to let you get by with identifying these qualities as masculine!

JACK: Perhaps you'll give me a dispensation if I report verbatim your caustic satirical response to why vigor, virility, and strength are considered masculine: "That's because women have been pictured as sweet little pansies growing beautifully in a safe sunny garden. We certainly couldn't have friendships that are virile, strong, and vigorous." I'm still trying to picture you as a sweet little pansy.

ANNE: Dialogical love eliminates all that garbage. In dialogical relationships each partner is sometimes strong and assertive and sometimes sympathetic and understanding. In dialogical love relationships, gender does not prescribe how partners respond to each other. They respond to each other as persons in mutual encounter—that's the essential meaning of dialogical love.

JACK: One reason for challenging traditional gendered relationships, other than their injustice to women, is that gendered prescriptions inhibit the development of dialogical love between the sexes.

ANNE: That's true of gendered categorical prescription, but aren't we also running the risk of making dialogical love a category that limits relationships and paradoxically makes dialogical love impersonal?

JACK: Not if we think of dialogical love as an enlightening term that directs us to the way we experience personal relationships rather than as a category that rigidly determines what counts as dialogical love and in the process prescribes it and makes it impersonal.

ANNE: Dialogical love can direct us to a quality of relationship potentially present in what is called love (Eros) and friendship. Love (Eros) and friendship, as used in our society, run the gamut from impersonal exploitive relationships to the most exalted of personal relationships. We need language that distinguishes the personal from the impersonal in human relationships. Our present language doesn't make that distinction.

JACK: Our use of dialogical love does. Dialogical love, as we use it, means love in which persons respond to each other as they are present to each other. This distinguishes it from impersonal "love" that uses others to satisfy sexual appetite, that loses the other in a cloud of romantic feeling, or rigidly follows culturally dictated ways of relating the sexes to each other.

ANNE: Interpreting friendship as dialogical love distinguishes it from impersonal colleague relationships, from functional-social relationships, and from Aristotle's lowest form of friendship based on usefulness to each other.

JACK: Dialogical love can also unite both friendships—face-to-face and side-by-side. Dialogical love refers to a quality of being in a relationship that can be expressed as either type of friendship.

ANNE: Couples do not have to choose either friendship or Eros, because in dialogical love, personal interaction fosters love for a person that can be expressed as both Eros and friendship. Personal love, experienced dialogically, is more than a quality that raises friendship and love to a higher level in the way Lewis and May interpret them.

JACK: Some couples we interviewed described dialogical love relationships even when they labeled them as a special kind of friendship. Those who recognized the inadequacy of friendship for describing their relationship sought other alternatives. Sue called her partner a "soul mate"; Jeanne and Russell, after struggling with the word *love*, recognized that their relationship was a different kind of love; and George, whom we interpreted poetically, affirmed that the distinction between lover and friend lost all meaning as his dialogical love relationship for Jane grew.

ANNE: The Mill's proudly proclaimed that their love was different from other loves because theirs was a free and equal dialogical relationship unaffected by sensuous feeling or so-called gender difference. The personal love relationship between C. S. Lewis and Joy eventually led him to reject his contention that love and friendship were different ways of being together and that men and women are basically different. After Joy's death, he claimed that only human arrogance could account for attributing certain virtues to men and others to women. The transformation in Lewis's thinking concerning the relationship of men and women and of love and friendship shows how relationships of dialogical love can lead persons to reach out for more adequate ways of articulating their relationship that challenge not only traditional ways but their own former views.

JACK: We experienced such a transformation. We first experienced dialogical love when I was startled by ecstasy that seemed to come from friendship rather than Eros. The only available terms for articulating what I was experiencing were *Eros* and *friendship*. Given those options, our ecstasy clearly came from friendship. I now believe that ecstasy came from dialogical love, unrecognized because it was unarticulated. That ecstasy came from experiencing personal love directly as dialogical love. Searching for the meaning of that direct experience of personal love eventually called us to write this book.

ANNE: We originally tried to cast our personal love as a friendship. We believed, like Lewis, that friendship should be considered a love, but we interpreted it as a face-to-face relationship, as May does. Then we called our way of being a "friend of friend" relationship to indicate that it was a friendship so special that our relationship, rather than a societal category, disclosed the full and profound meaning of our being friends. But I believe that we were trying to stretch the meaning of friendship in order to avoid saying we loved each other.

JACK: Our experience of love, as well as that of others, did not fit any sociocultural categories that we knew. It didn't fit friendship or Eros, even when they were interpreted as personal love, as Lewis and May do. It was experienced as abundant being rather than as instances of Eros, friendship, or other articulated relationships. At first, we were confidant that we could describe how abundant being came from personal interaction and show how that experience could be articulated as personal love with the help of Buber, Macmurray, and Schutz.

ANNE: But we thought we would only be able to articulate it as personal love. We were startled to discover that the key to unlocking the meaning of our relationship was dialogical love in which personal love could be experienced directly rather than as a quality of Eros and friendship.

JACK: In our society personal love, at best, is recognized as a quality that can raise Eros and friendship to a higher level. But it is rarely recognized as love in its own right that can be experienced directly as dialogical love. When personal love is given its due, then the much heralded claim that we must choose between love (Eros) and friendship makes no sense. Those who love each other dialogically develop relationships that foster abundant being without interference from cultural prescriptions.

ANNE: The cultural terms of *friend* and *lover* often inhibit persons in our society from recognizing the full meaning of personal love. When personal love is disclosed, most people ask, "Are they friends or lovers?" Instead of labeling, why don't they respond to that disclosure directly by saying, "Isn't it wonderful that they love each other!"

JACK: Perhaps that response will become possible now that we have publicly reflected on the meaning of relationships such as ours. We have discovered that in dialogical love personal love can be experienced as love in its own right without being articulated as a quality that elevates friendship and lover relationships.

ANNE: Then one answer to the question, "Why dialogical love?" is that it calls for experiencing personal love directly rather than as a friendship or lover relationship or as a man and woman

relationship. Dialogical love also well articulates love relationships directly as I-Thou relationships rather than categorically
as I-It relationships, as personal love rather than societal, and as
we-relationships rather than societally determined relationships.
Finally, it articulates the various relationships we have considered that have been misdirected and limited by traditional categories defining the relationships of men and women.

JACK: We could well conclude the book with your summary answer
to the question, "Why dialogical love?" But we need to speak
briefly to the professional and personal goals stated in the first
chapter.

ANNE: First, let's consider our professional goals. We hope that our
quest to make sense of personal love relationships as dialogical
love will encourage other scholars to explore and articulate personal love relationships between the sexes without limiting them
to traditional Eros and friend relationships. We further hope
that our study will encourage others to blend personal experience with scholarly treatments concerning personal relationships
and to include personal dialogue in their quest for meaning.

JACK: We believe that our study suggests that social scientists consider
the implications of our finding that humans are called into abundant being by dialogical love relationships with other persons.
This finding challenges the egology that Kunz contends domi-
nates psychology and prevents serious consideration of responsible care of human beings for each other. Other issues that
need to be pursued are the implications of dialogical love for
courtship and marriage, for relationships between heterosexual
and homosexual persons, for same-sex relationships that do and
do not involve Eros.

ANNE: Now to our personal goal. We have issued a call for men and
women to go beyond the cultural prescriptions of friend and
lover by entering a radically personal way of being. In this dialogical relationship persons respond directly, freely, and authen-
tically to the presence of each other. These relationships cultivate
personal love that fosters abundant being and we-relationships
that constitute a shared world and destiny. We hope we have

encouraged men and women to pursue dialogical love relationships that foster abundant being—relationships that silently
emerge from cultivating free, equal, open, and spontaneous personal relationships between the sexes, unfettered by cultural
prescriptions.

REFERENCES

Aristotle. *Nicomachean Ethics.* Translated by W. D. Ross. In *The Basic Works of Aristotle,* edited by R. McKeon. New York: Random House, 1941.

Bergoffen, Debra B. *The Philosophy of Simone de Beauvoir.* Albany, NY: State University of New York Press, 1997.

Berkson, Dorothy. "'Born and Bred in Different Nations: Margaret Fuller and Ralph Waldo Emerson." In *Patrons and Proteges: Gender, Friendship, and Writing in Nineteenth-Century America,* edited by Shirley Marchalonis, pp. 3–30. New Brunswick: Rutgers University Press, 1988.

Buber, Martin. *I and Thou.* Translated by Walter Kaufmann. New York: Charles Scribner's Sons, 1970.

Cahill, Thomas. *How the Irish Saved Civilization.* New York: Nan A. Talese Doubleday, 1995.

Dorsett, Lyle W. *Joy and C. S. Lewis: The Story of an Extraordinary Marriage.* London: HarperCollins, 1993.

Eliot, T. S. *The Elder Statesman.* New York: Farrar, Straus and Cudahy, 1959.

Elkins, Leigh E., and Peterson, "Christopher. Gender Differences in Best Friendships." *Sex Roles* 29 (1993):497–508.

Emerson, Ralph Waldo. *The Letters of Ralph Waldo Emerson.* Vol. 2. Edited by Ralph L. Rusk. New York: Columbia University Press, 1939.

———. *The Best of Ralph Waldo Emerson.* Edited by Gordon S. Haight. Toronto: D. Van Nostrand, 1941.

Friedman, Maurice. "Martin Buber's Philosophy of Education." *Educational Theory* 6 (April 1956):95.

Fuller, Margaret. *The Letters of Margaret Fuller*. Vols. 1 & 2. Edited by Robert N. Hudspeth. Ithaca: Cornell University Press, 1983.

Gendlin, Eugene T. *Focusing*, 2nd ed. New York: Bantam Books, 1981.

Gray, John. *Men Are from Mars; Women Are from Venus*. New York: Harper-Collins, 1992.

Hayek, F. A. *John Stuart Mill and Harriet Taylor: Their Correspondence and Subsequent Marriage*. Chicago: University of Chicago Press, 1951, quoted in Phyllis Rose, *Parallel Lives*, p. 112. New York: Vintage Books, 1983.

Kunz, George. *The Paradox of Power and Weakness*. Albany: State University of New York Press, 1998.

Lewis, C. S. *Surprised by Joy: The Shape of My Early Life*. New York: Harcourt Brace, 1955.

———. *The Four Loves*. New York: Harcourt Brace Jovanovich, 1960.

———. *A Grief Observed*. New York: Bantam Books, 1976.

Macmurray, John. *Reason and Emotion*. Atlantic Highlands, NJ: Humanities Press, 1935.

May, Rollo. *Love and Will*. New York: W. W. Norton, 1969.

Meilaender, Gilbert. *The Taste for the Other: The Social and Ethical Thought of C. S. Lewis*. Grand Rapids, Michigan: William B. Eerdmans, 1978.

———. *Friendship: A Study in Theological Ethics*. Notre Dame, Indiana: University of Notre Dame Press, 1981.

———. "When Harry & Sally Read the *Nicomachean Ethics*: Friendship between Men and Women." In *The Changing Face of Friendship*, edited by Leroy S. Rouner. Notre Dame, Indiana: University of Notre Dame Press, 1994.

Mill, John Stuart. *The Subjection of Women*. Edited by Sue Mansfield. Arlington Heights, IL: AHM Publishing, 1980.

———. *The Autobiography of John Stuart Mill*. New York. Columbia University Press, 1924.

———. *The Early Draft of John Stuart Mill's Autobiography*. Edited by Jack Stillinger. Urbana: University of Illinois Press, 1961.

My Best Friend's Wedding. Director P. J. Hogan. Producer Jerry Zucker. 105 min. Videocassette. Columbia Tristar, 1997.

Natanson, Maurice. *Anonymity: A Study in the Philosophy of Alfred Schutz.* Bloomington: Indiana University Press, 1986.

Nicholson, William. *Shadowlands: A Drama.* New York: Samuel French, 1989.

Nozick, Robert. *The Examined Life.* New York: Simon and Schuster, 1989.

Plato. *Symposium.* In *The Collected Dialogues of Plato.* Edited by Edith Hamilton and Huntington Cairns. Princeton, NJ: Princeton University Press, 1961.

Priestley, J. B. *Talking: An Essay,* pp. 63ff, 97. New York: Harper & Brothers, 1926. Quoted in Gilbert Meilaender, "When Harry & Sally Read *Nicomachean Ethics*: Friendship between Men and Women." In *The Changing Face of Friendship,* pp. 192–193, edited by Leroy Rouner. Notre Dame, Indiana: University of Notre Dame Press, 1994.

Rose, Phyllis. *Parallel Lives: Five Victorian Marriages.* New York: Vintage Books, 1983.

Rubin, Lillian B. *Just Friends: The Role of Friendship in Our Lives.* New York: Harper & Row, 1985.

Same Time Next Year. Directed by Robert Mulligan. 119 min. Universal Studies Home Video, 1978.

Schutz, Alfred. *The Phenomenology of the Social World.* Translated by George Walsh and Frederick Lehnert. Chicago: Northwestern University Press, 1967.

Simon, Caroline J. Can Men and Women be Friends? *The Christian Century* 114 (1997a):188–194.

———. *The Disciplined Heart: Love, Destiny & Imagination.* Grand Rapids, Michigan: William B. Eerdmans, 1997b.

Solomon, Robert C. *Love: Emotion, Myth, and Metaphor.* New York: Anchor Press/Doubleday, 1981.

———. *About Love: Reinventing Romance and Our Times.* New York: Simon and Schuster, 1988.

Stegner, Wallace. *Crossing to Safety.* New York: Penguin Books, 1987.

Walsh, Chad. Afterword. In C. S. Lewis. *A Grief Observed.* New York: Bantam Books, 1976.

Werking, Kathy. *We're Just Good Friends: Women and Men in Nonromantic Relationships.* New York: Guilford Press, 1997.

West, Ken. Seize the Moment When a Door Opens. *The News & Advance,* 25 December 1977.

When Harry Met Sally. Director Rob Reiner. Castle Rock Entertainment, 1989.

Whitney, Catherine. *Uncommon Lives: Gay Men and Straight Women.* New York: New American Library, 1990.

Young, Iris Marion. *Throwing Like a Girl and Other Essays in Feminist Philosophy and Social Theory.* Bloomington: Indiana University Press, 1990.

Zaner, Richard. *The Context of Self.* Athens, Ohio: Ohio University Press, 1981.

INDEX

127